STRATEGIES
FOR THE
1980s

A FREEDOM HOUSE BOOK

Strategies for the 1980s: Lessons of Cuba, Vietnam, and Afghanistan
Philip van Slyck
STUDIES IN FREEDOM, NUMBER 1

STRATEGIES
FOR THE
1980s

Lessons of Cuba, Vietnam, and Afghanistan

Philip van Slyck

Foreword by Daniel P. Moynihan

STUDIES IN FREEDOM, NUMBER 1

GREENWOOD PRESS
Westport, Connecticut

Library of Congress Cataloging in Publication Data

Van Slyck, Philip.
  Strategies for the 1980s

  (Studies in freedom, ISSN 0273-1231; no. 1)
(A Freedom House book)
  Bibliography: p.
  Includes index.
  1. United States—Military policy. 2. United
States—Foreign relations—1977–   . 3. World
politics—1975–1985. I. Title. II. Series:
Studies in freedom; no. 1. III. Series: Freedom
House book.
UA23.V29   355'.033073   81-4627
ISBN 0-313-22975-9   AACR2

Library of Congress Catalog Card Number: 81-4627
ISBN: 0-313-22975-9
ISSN: 0273-1231

First published in 1981

Greenwood Press
A division of Congressional Information Service, Inc.
88 Post Road West, Westport, Connecticut 06881

Printed in the United States of America

10 9 8 7 6 5 4 3 2 1

Freedom House Books

The Freedom House Book series is directed by Freedom House, a national nongovernmental organization founded in 1941, that seeks to strengthen free institutions in the United States and abroad.

It conducts, as one of its major activities, the year-round Comparative Survey of Freedom, assessing the level of political rights and civil liberties in every country and territory. The Survey's findings are published annually in the organization's bimonthly of current affairs, *Freedom at Issue*, and, in fuller form, in its yearbook, *Freedom in the World: Political Rights and Civil Liberties*. A division of Freedom House is the Center for Appeals for Freedom, which receives, and distributes in English translation, the writing of dissenters in oppressive countries of the political left and right where free expression is curtailed.

Freedom House traditionally engages in research and issues advisories on important foreign and domestic policy questions. All its programs are directed by fifty trustees who play leading roles in journalism, trade unions, corporate management, government, and the universities.

The supreme task of world politics is not the prevention of war but a satisfactory organization of mankind.

Walter Lippmann,
The Stakes of Diplomacy, 1915

Contents

Foreword

YEARS AGO, toward the end of the decade itself, the late Richard Hofstadter described the 1960s as an "age of rubbish." He found "almost the entire intellectual community . . . lost in dissent." There was almost no dialogue left "between those who are alienated from society and those who are prepared to make an intelligent defense of it." Nor did he think we could talk or write or think our way out of that impasse. He judged that an extraordinary *event* would have to take place for that spell to be broken. He looked back at the Molotov-Ribbentrop Pact of 1939 as the event that broke the spell of the 1930s.

It was a long time coming, but it begins to appear that the Soviet invasion of Afghanistan in the very last days of the 1970s was the event that Hofstadter had judged necessary to break the spell of the 1960s. All of a sudden the nature of the Soviet threat to world stability became clear to almost everyone in the United States, as did the startlingly limited power of the United States to counter that threat.

There was, of course, a relationship between these two facts (or, rather, sets of facts), and for those who did not discern it, help came from a somewhat unusual Soviet source. A few months after the Afghanistan invasion Mr. Ilya Dzhirkvelov, a KGB officer seconded to the World Health Organization as an information officer, defected to Britain. In an interview with *The Times* Mr. Dzhirkvelov explained that he and his colleagues in Geneva saw the invasion and occupation as "proof of the contempt of the Soviet leadership for the United States president and world opinion." The Politburo, he continued, "wanted to test Western reaction, to see how far they could go before the West took firm action in response, up to and including military action." And, of course, they got an answer of sorts. In his State of the Union address twenty-six days after Soviet troops entered Kabul the president of the United States drew a line in the Persian Gulf and declared that we would defend it.

But how? In particular, how, when forced, to do so without escalating to general nuclear war? This aspect of the Carter Doctrine is not much attended to just now; it is shock enough that all at once a president is talking about war of any kind, and indeed war with the USSR. Clearly there is yet a good deal of thinking through to be done!

This is the effort (by no means limited to military issues) to which Philip van Slyck directs this concise and clarifying memorandum. He puts the matter straight out:

Outraged American public reaction to the Soviet invasion of Afghanistan, and the attention the public paid to the defense-preparedness issue in the 1980 election campaign, suggest that the American people may now be ready to make up for lost time, provided there were a working consensus on the measures possible and necessary to meet the challenge. There is not yet such a consensus.

There is ample blame to be shared, he writes, but asks that we direct our energies to what can be learned as against who can be accused. He looks to the lessons of Cuba and Vietnam (that "ill-starred, mismanaged, and ultimately humiliating national ordeal"). He describes the "generation of peace" euphoria that ironically followed that humiliation, and now the harsh intrusion of reality.

It is astonishing, this transformation; and it may have come too quickly for its lesson to be absorbed. At one point in his argument Mr. van Slyck cites the matter-of-fact pronouncement of Secretary of Defense Harold Brown in his Annual Report to Congress for fiscal year 1981: "There can be no doubt about the steady increase in the Soviet defense effort each year for more than fifteen years." It is now a quarter to half again as great as the American effort (whose recent tendency van Slyck nicely calls the "build-down"). And of course the secretary felt our effort must be correspondingly increased.

Now this is the same defense intellectual who as an adviser in the 1976 presidential campaign shaped the pledge that, if elected, Jimmy Carter would *cut* the United States defense budget. The facts that Dr. Brown cited in 1980 were equally available to him in 1976—yet were rejected in the one year, much as they were embraced in the other.

It is not only our military strength that we have "built down." Too many have forgotten the force of liberal ideas. There was a time when we single-mindedly cultivated the means of propagating them, and it made a difference. Mr. van Slyck reminds us that Solzhenitsyn himself has described our radio broadcasts into the Soviet Union as "the mightiest weapon the United States possesses to create mutual understanding (or even an alliance) between America and the oppressed Russian people." This weapon, no less than our armed strength, is in decay.

How so? Because even the most formidable minds are capable of profound delusion in this area. It is difficult; it is painful;

it is not always politically advantageous to recognize our predicament. Any form of avoidance, much less euphoria, exerts a profound attraction. The more rare and to be valued, then, is the work of a learned and disciplined student of international affairs whose dedication to the great liberal truths, *and* to reality howsoever harsh, has served him in an already distinguished career, and promises to make an even greater contribution in the critical period on which we are now entered. We are in his debt.

DANIEL P. MOYNIHAN
UNITED STATES SENATOR

Acknowledgments

THIS MONOGRAPH grew out of various discussions among members of the board of trustees, executive committee, and staff of Freedom House, as we debated the appropriate American policy responses to the Soviet power challenge in the weeks following the brutal invasion of Afghanistan. Several of us had further exchanges as the 1980 presidential campaign heated up, and I was encouraged to draft my own views for publication. I did so, delaying the completion of the manuscript until after the election, in order to address it to the incoming Administration.

On a number of occasions during the year I benefited from the suggestions, corrections, and counsel of colleagues, none of whom I am sure wishes to be blamed for views and policy recommendations which are exclusively my own responsibility. Nor, despite the fact that it is issued as a Freedom House Book, does this essay speak for the organization.

Nonetheless, I wish to express my personal indebtedness for their contributions to my understanding to the following Freedom House colleagues in particular: Clifford P. Case, chairman; John Richardson, Jr., president; Leo Cherne, honorary chairman; trustees William R. Kintner, Howland H. Sargeant, and the late Allard K. Lowenstein; Leonard R. Sussman, executive director; Raymond D. Gastil, director of the Comparative Survey of Freedom; and, for their cheerfulness and competence in managing the production of this project, Patricia A. McCormack and Mrs. Jessie Miller.

I should also like to thank for their valuable editorial suggestions my good friend Professor Charles A. Hogan, formerly of the University of California and Drew University; my wise colleague in earlier endeavors, Professor Edward A. Lutz of Cornell University; and my valued professional associate, David T. Lemon.

PvS

STRATEGIES
FOR THE
1980s

I   Afghanistan as Watershed

FUTURE HISTORIANS may quibble with President Jimmy Carter's assessment of the December 1979 Soviet invasion of Afghanistan as "the most serious threat to peace since the Second World War." Yet none will deny the event was a watershed, arresting the momentum of a decade of détente, putting the Strategic Arms Limitations Talks (SALT) on indefinite hold, and almost instantly recreating a broad national consensus in support of accelerated U.S. defense spending.

Moreover, the question whether the United States possesses the military means and political will to compete more assertively with the Soviet Union on the global stage—and if not, who is to blame and who is best qualified to remedy the deficiencies—became one of the critical issues in the 1980 election campaign. This issue, combined with economic and other voter dissatisfactions, contributed in November 1980 to the rejection of the Carter Administration, loss of Democratic control of the Senate, erosion of the Democratic majority in the House of Representatives, and the landslide electoral victory of President Ronald Reagan.

The new Administration begins its term with a clear popular mandate to overhaul American strategies and rebuild American capabilities for meeting a broad range of international challenges which the continuing Soviet repression in Afghanistan, and Soviet intimidation of Poland, have forced into focus. What remains to be negotiated by the new leadership is a fresh compact with the people, setting forth the national purposes and strategies, the reordered national priorities, and the risks and costs entailed in repairing America's sense that it is a principal actor, rather than reactor, in the great events that are shaping current and future history.

Terms of that compact were merely implied, never spelled out, in the political rhetoric of the campaign. The national policy debate which must now begin is potentially the most far-reaching in its consequences—for the United States and for the world—since the early postwar national debate which defined for the first time the role of the United States as paramount world power. The policy outcomes of this new debate should define whether, how, and for what ends that role will be continued in the 1980s and beyond.

Initial Response to the Threat

The Soviet invasion of Afghanistan, with an estimated 85,000 troops, was the first instance since the closing months of World War II when the USSR used its own military forces to seize control of another state outside the tacitly conceded boundaries of Soviet hegemony. The invasion was not unheralded. The Soviet Union had had a role in the political coup in Afghanistan twenty months earlier, in April 1978. The 1979 invasion replaced that pro-Soviet regime with a more reliable puppet and superimposed direct Soviet control over the entire Afghan civil and military apparatus.

The Carter Administration viewed the invasion, not only as naked aggression against the Afghan people, but also as a possible positioning of Soviet forces for a more ambitious assault against vital interests of the United States and its democratic allies. Specifically, the Administration was concerned about a future Soviet move to interdict U.S., North American Treaty Organization (NATO), and Japanese access to the essential oil supplies of the Persian (or Arab) Gulf region.

It was on these grounds that President Carter declared in his State of the Union message to Congress in January 1980 that any outside effort "to gain control" of the Gulf region "will be regarded as an assault on the vital interests of the United States" and "will be repelled by any means necessary, including military force." This declaration, quickly dubbed the Carter Doctrine, was followed by a series of specific responses.

At the United Nations, U.S. Ambassador Donald F. McHenry orchestrated the outrage of virtually the entire noncommunist world in an overwhelming General Assembly vote of condemnation, and demand for withdrawal of Soviet troops, following Soviet veto of a more potent Security Council vote to the same effect.

The Administration shelved its request for Senate consent to ratification of the SALT II treaty—which had little chance of passing, anyhow—and sought, with mixed results, the cooperation of allies and nonaligned nations in punishing the Soviet Union through selected trade restraints (including an embargo on new U.S. grain sales) and a boycott of the 1980 Moscow Summer Olympics.

Most important, U.S. defense capabilities, following more than a decade of attrition, were to be rebuilt at an accelerated rate. Since the United States did not at the beginning of 1980 possess adequate military forces in the Middle East to undertake any sizable and sustained military operations, much less to "repel" a Soviet thrust to seize control of the Gulf, the immediate priority was to establish tactical naval and air superiority in the Gulf vicinity. This entailed borrowing combat-ready units from other theaters, negotiating right of access for U.S. forces to stategically positioned bases on friendly territory in the region, and quiet recruitment of NATO naval units for back-up support in the Arabian Sea. This build-up continued through spring and summer.

When war between Iraq and Iran broke out in September 1980, posing a more immediate threat to oil supplies from the Gulf, the United States had on station in the area naval task forces capable of keeping the sea lanes open and of preventing either belligerent from closing the Strait of Hormuz, through which 60 percent of the world's oil trade moves. The U.S. Navy's Middle East Force, on patrol in the Gulf, had the back-up of combined U.S., British, and French naval forces in the Arabian Sea, including one of the largest warships afloat, the *Dwight D. Eisenhower*, a multipurpose aircraft carrier. This powerful assembly provided two-to-one superiority over Soviet warships in the region.

However, these U.S. naval forces had to be drawn down from other potential crisis areas, including the Indian Ocean and the Western Pacific. Moreover, in the event of a widening of the Iraq-Iran conflict, or the threat of intervention by Soviet ground forces in Iran or elsewhere in the Gulf, the United States still lacked adequate ground forces for "rapid deployment" in the area. Units for this purpose would have to be assembled from combat-ready Army and Marine forces in Western Europe and the continental United States. An estimated 100,000 reservists would have to be called up to man the extended supply lines, and civilian aircraft would probably have to be commandeered to deploy the fighting units on a timely schedule and to sustain them.

Carter's secretary of defense, Harold Brown, acknowledged that it could take $5 billion a year over five years to create an effective rapid-deployment force, provide it with adequate transport, build up the forward bases it will require, and stockpile the heavy equipment and other supplies that would be needed for combat operations.[1] In November 1980 Army Chief of Staff General Edward C. Meyer called for an additional $40 billion over five years to build the army into a flexible and mobile global fighting force.

For the next several years, in other words, the oil-based American and allied economies will continue to be vulnerable to a takeover, cutoff, or shutdown of the Gulf oil fields, whether by wars or revolutions involving the Gulf states, or, especially, by a determined Soviet effort to seize control of the Gulf. During this same period, the United States would be equally hard put, should the need arise, to project adequate military power into other potential crisis areas such as Pakistan, on the Afghan border, or Thailand, a U.S. treaty partner under pressure from 200,000 Soviet-equipped Vietnamese troops occupying Cambodia.

Inadequate U.S. *conventional military capabilities* to meet new challenges to important U.S. interests, or to treaty commitments, is but one dimension of the current U.S. predicament. In addition, the credibility of the U.S. *strategic nuclear deterrent* is increasingly suspect because of U.S. failure to respond earlier to a long-term Soviet build-up of strategic weaponry.[2] This build-up includes increasingly accurate intercontinental missiles which threaten U.S. land-based retaliatory missiles in their North American silos, as well as the new Soviet SS-20 mobile missiles with MIRVed warheads, now being deployed against Western European targets.[3]

U.S. and allied efforts to stabilize the balance in strategic weapons will also take time to mature. The proposed U.S. mobile land-based MX missile, intended to remedy the growing vulnerability of fixed U.S. land-based missiles, cannot be deployed before 1985 at the earliest. The new generation of U.S. intermediate-range missiles, which NATO voted to accept in December 1979 as a counter to the SS-20, and the land-based U.S. cruise missile for basing in Western Europe, will not begin to be deployed before 1983.

During the early 1980s, in other words, the United States will lack adequate conventional military capabilities to enforce the Carter Doctrine in the Gulf region. Nor in this same period of instability and risk will the United States have a fully credible capability of threatening to resort to nuclear war in defense of the Gulf. This is the "window" of vulnerability which has concerned numerous defense specialists in both political parties.

The most meaningful measure of an *offensive* military advantage is whether force can be applied, either through political intimidation and blackmail, or through direct military action, to achieve a strategic gain over an adversary, and whether that net gain can be accomplished with impunity. The corresponding measure of a *defensive* military advantage is whether adequate power is in place to deny an adversary those options— adequate power, that is, to deter, repel, or punish the adversary's adventure. In both senses, the United States clearly had the overwhelming edge in Cuba in 1962; the Soviet Union, if it chooses to employ the land and air power available to it, appears to have the edge, offensively as well as defensively, in Southwest Asia today, despite U.S. tactical naval superiority in the Gulf and the Arabian Sea.

Proximity of Afghanistan and the Gulf states to the USSR's borders is of course an important Soviet logistical advantage, as was the proximity of Cuba to U.S. shores nineteen years ago. The decisive U.S. advantage then was the assured conventional capability of "taking out" the Cuban-based Soviet missiles before they could be made operational, with or without an invasion of Cuba. In addition, as insurance against nuclear blackmail, the United States had a five- or six-to-one numerical superiority in ICBMs capable of striking military, industrial, and civilian targets inside the Soviet Union. That U.S. edge has since disappeared, as the Soviet Union has deployed more numerous and heavier missiles (i.e., capable of carrying more warheads per missile), although the USSR is still far from achieving the margin of superiority the United States maintained until the late 1960s.

Assessing the Dangers

It would be as unproductive to exaggerate as it would be dangerous to underestimate Soviet military advantages, actual or anticipated, during 1980–85. Western experts honestly disagree about what Soviet theoreticians call the "correlation of forces," or military power balance, and what this implies for Soviet freedom of action to impose its political will by force or by nuclear blackmail. Nonetheless, as long as the actual U.S.-Soviet gap in conventional military capabilities is so wide in areas of potential confrontation, such as Southwest Asia, and as long as the balance in strategic capabilities is so narrow, it could prove a perilous luxury to rely on pacific Soviet "intentions." A deterrent which is not fully credible may provide the temptation for political if not military challenge.

For the Reagan Administration and the American people, the most pressing task is a reshaping of foreign-policy assumptions and priorities, not simply to respond to current crises and near-future vulnerabilities, but also to insure that the United States will not again fall into so dangerous a predicament that vital American and allied interests, and the stability of the global power balance, are or appear to be in peril. This will entail, in addition to careful assessment of current dangers, a reexamination of those failures of past American perceptions and policies which have made the current threats possible and may even have invited them. Without clearer understanding of the long prologue to the present crisis, the scope, pace, and endurance of America's response may be inadequate to prevent further deterioration of the security of the United States and of the alliance of democracies.

Soviet mischief-making in Iranian and Arab politics has been highly visible throughout the postwar era, beginning with its brief postwar military occupation of northern Iran and including its costly support of Arab arms in the last three Arab-Israeli wars. Starting in the mid-1970s, as Soviet conventional and strategic power have rapidly grown, Soviet opportunism has become bolder. This boldness has been demonstrated in overt Soviet, and Soviet-proxy, support for Marxist-led guerrillas in southern Africa and for pro-Soviet regimes in Ethiopia and South Yemen, at the Arabian Sea portals to the Red Sea and the Suez Canal. By the late 1970s, it was not far-fetched to postulate a Soviet strategy of straddling U.S. and allied access to absolutely essential raw materials—

southern African chrome, cobalt, and manganese, and Middle Eastern oil.[4]

To the extent the United States is responsible for its own present predicament in the Gulf region, the errors of judgment and policy have not all been recent ones. Three major errors were long-time American complacency about its oil dependence on the region; excessive U.S. reliance on the Shah of Iran to maintain stability in the region; and an across-the-board decline in relative U.S. military power, especially in the aftermath of Vietnam.

Moreover, the vulnerability of U.S. stakes and the dilemmas of U.S. diplomacy in the region are as much the product of long-festering indigenous tensions and instabilities as of Soviet opportunism in exploiting those disintegrative forces. Three decades of intractable Arab-Israeli hostility, marked by four wars and chronic terrorism, as well as by bitter divisions among Arab leaderships, contribute to the American burden and invite Soviet aggravation.

There have been other recent and violent events in the area which neither the United States nor the Soviet Union could prevent or control, but which nonetheless injured U.S. interests and impaired U.S. freedom of action. These events included the toppling of the Shah of Iran (whose role as "policeman" of the Gulf the Nixon Administration had surrogated, and the Nixon, Ford, and Carter Administrations had lavishly supported); the U.S. embassy seizure and taking of American diplomatic hostages in Teheran; desecration and temporary occupation of the Grand Mosque at Mecca by Moslem fanatics; mob sacking of the U.S. embassies in Islamabad and Tripoli while Pakistani and Libyan authorities stood by; and the outbreak of a shooting war between Iraq and Iran.

The cumulative effect of these developments has been to inform the American people of their dependence, in the broadest meaning of national security, on socially unstable and politically fragile states reaching from southern and northeastern Africa, through the Middle East, and across southern Asia, a region Carter's national security assistant, Zbigniew Brzezinski, once called an "arc of crisis." An American strategy which focuses solely on Soviet military challenges along this arc, while neglecting indigenous social ferment and political rivalries, offers no lasting security for U.S. interests in the area.

Indeed, a classic Soviet military thrust to seize and hold the Gulf oil fields is but one way (and, considering the risks, the least likely way) for the Soviet Union to cut off Western access to the oil. The Soviet role was at best marginal in promoting the two most disruptive recent events in the region, the Shiite revolution in Iran and the Iraq-Iran war, although both events may have expanded Soviet opportunities for meddling. The most the Soviet Union might have to do to constrict Western oil supplies more drastically (were this its intention) would be to promote and support covertly in other Gulf states the best-organized and best-led underground movements—whether Marxist, religious-fundamentalist, separatist, or terrorist—willing to accept Soviet help. Once in power, under the strong hint of Soviet protection, these forces could be expected to be as hostile as revolutionary Iran to U.S. interests.

In this context, the conjunction of the hostage seizure in Iran and the Soviet invasion of Afghanistan complicated greatly the tasks of crisis management for the United States. In terms of humane concern for the hostages, national *amour-propre*, and domestic politics, Iran and the Carter Administration's handling of the hostage crisis tended to dominate American public attention throughout 1980. In geopolitical terms of allied security and world peace, however, the far more urgent concern of the public and its leadership should be the global power challenge represented by the continuing Soviet military repression of Afghanistan and the progressively deeper Soviet involvement in the volatile politics of the Middle East and other vulnerable areas of the third world, including Latin America and the Caribbean.

One aspect of that challenge is whether and how the Soviet Union can be induced to withdraw its troops and to restore Afghanistan's sovereignty, an objective the United States and its allies are ill-equipped to accomplish by military pressure, and have so far showed little promise of achieving by diplomacy, despite broad Islamic and other third-world support for this objective.

A second aspect of the challenge is how the United States and its allies can contribute most effectively to the political stabilization of the independent states that constitute the critical arc, promoting the common interest in socioeconomic and political evolution, rather than revolution and disintegration. Unrest and upheaval serve the interests only of indigenous extremists and the Soviet Union. It is imperative, for example, that the United States continue its efforts to promote a just and durable Arab-Israeli peace settlement, including an acceptable formula for Palestinian self-determination and permanent borders. Such a settlement could contribute substantially to the repairing of U.S. political and security relations with the principal Islamic powers in the region, including, ultimately, Iran.

A third aspect of the challenge, inseparable from the global Soviet challenge, is to overcome in quick and orderly fashion those deficiencies in military power and presence which now severely limit American ability to protect vital allied interests in the region.

More than a year after the Soviet invasion of Afghanistan and the pronouncement of the Carter Doctrine, U.S. conventional military capabilities in the Gulf region are adequate to accomplish three of the four missions the Pentagon contemplates in that area: to prevent a regional power from closing the Hormuz Strait or interrupting the flow of oil from the major oil-producing states; to seize and protect major oil fields from saboteurs or terrorists; and, on request, to assist a friendly state, such as Saudi Arabia, to maintain or restore internal order. The United States still lacks the assured capablity of deterring or repelling a hypothetical Soviet invasion of, for example, Iran or Pakistan. There is speculation that the closest the United States will be able to come in the next year or two to fulfilling that fourth mission would be to preempt a Soviet thrust by sending a trip-wire ground force, presumably airborne, to force Soviet leaders to consider the risks of direct hostile contact with American troops.

Notes

1. The Soviet Union is also known to be "prepositioning" tanks, aircraft, other advanced weapons, and communications systems in Libya, Syria, Ethiopia, and South Yemen.

2. In 1977, according to the U.S. Arms Control and Disarmament Agency, Soviet military spending at $140 billion represented one third of global military spending. The United States ranked second at $101 billion, followed by China ($35 billion), West Germany ($16.3 billion), and France ($14.8 billion). NATO and Warsaw Pact military expenditures were about equal, at approximately $164 billion.

3. MIRV: Multiple Independently targeted Reentry Vehicles, equipping a single rocket to attack a number of widely separated

targets. For "planning purposes," Secretary Brown told the Naval War College at Newport, Rhode Island, on August 20, 1980: "We must assume that the ICBM [land-based Intercontinental Ballistic Missile] leg of our triad could be destroyed within a very short time as one result of a Soviet surprise attack." However, he discounted the likelihood of such a counterforce strike, since the other two legs of the U.S. triad—submarine-launched missiles and strategic bombers—would survive and would be capable of devastating retaliation.

4. By the mid-1980s, CIA studies predict, and recent Soviet data tend to confirm, the Soviet Union will become a net importer of oil and potentially a dangerous competitor for Persian Gulf oil supplies.

II Origins of the U.S. Predicament

THE PRECARIOUS power balance in which the United States now finds itself results primarily from the failure to keep pace in power and strategy, during the past fifteen years, with the Soviet Union's unremitting arms build-up and global projection of its power for Soviet political purposes.

Functionally, the U.S. handicap lies, first, in the balance of strategic forces needed to *insure beyond doubt* the credibility of the U.S. deterrent (i.e., assurance that the Soviet Union will not risk a military assault against the United States or its allies because of the clear U.S. capacity to survive such an attack and to inflict unacceptable retaliatory damage on the Soviet Union) and, second, the conventional military power and mobility to deter or counter localized Soviet threats to U.S. and allied interests, such as the present implied threat to the Gulf, without having to escalate to general nuclear war.[1]

How seriously the actual balance in military power has deteriorated in fifteen years is difficult to quantify. The gap in relative U.S. and Soviet defense spending during that period can be approximated, however.

Defense share of the U.S. National budget was 46 percent in 1964, prior to the Vietnam build-up. By 1977, following the

Vietnam withdrawal and in the final budget of the Gerald R.
Ford Administration, it had declined to 23 percent. In relation
to GNP, the decline was from 8 percent to 5.2 percent. In real
terms, adjusting for inflation, the 1978 defense budget was
about equal to the 1964 budget in what it could buy. In comparison, growth in Soviet defense spending has been steady since the
mid-1960s, as Secretary Brown stated in his Annual Report to
Congress for fiscal 1981:

There can be no doubt about the steady increase in the Soviet defense
effort each year for more than fifteen years. As the Soviet gross
national product has grown, so has the defense effort. Its annual rate of
increase has averaged more than three percent measured by what it
would cost the United States to duplicate that effort in our economy,
and between four and five percent measured in rubles. By how much
the present effort now exceeds our own is less certain. It could be by as
much as 45 percent, or as little as 25 percent.

Such comparisons are of course imprecise. U.S. and Soviet
costs—for weapons research and development, and manufacturing, or for personnel and administration—are not comparable. Neither is the quality of technology appropriate and available to each side's military missions. Some of the most advanced
U.S. technologies—the "stealth" technology for equipping aircraft and missiles to penetrate Soviet radar undetected, preci-
sion guidance for various types of warheads, antitank weaponry, and reconnaissance capabilities, for example—may not
be presently accessible to the Soviets at any cost. In other
areas—chemical biological, and antisatellite warfare, and
antiballistic-missile systems, for example—the Soviet Union
may currently have the lead, in hardware if not in technology.
Symmetry between the opposing defense establishments—in
forces, in weapons, or even in levels of defense spending—

is not, in other words, an adequate measure of a stable balance. It is, in fact, a legitimate and extremely complicated debate whether, by how much, and for what purposes the currently planned increases in defense spending should be increased further, including the question of how much to allocate for new hardware and how much for manpower and training.

It is generally agreed among experts, however, including congressional military specialists of both parties, that the relative U.S. position in the global power balance has deteriorated dangerously and that the process has been under way since the 1960s. In the first volume of his memoirs, former Secretary of State Henry A. Kissinger suggests that the turning point was the 1962 Cuban missile crisis, a "great American victory" from which "the American and Soviet governments drew diametrically opposite conclusions." Following the Soviet withdrawal from Cuba, Kissinger writes, U.S. policy turned "to the pursuit of arms control and détente" and a unilateral ceiling on the deployment of American ICBMs. The quite different Soviet response to the humiliating Cuban experience was summed up in the remark of Soviet diplomat Vasily V. Kuznetsov to U.S. negotiator John J. McCloy, which Kissinger cites: "You Americans will never be able to do this to us again!" The Soviet Union, according to Kissinger, "thereupon launched itself on a determined, systematic, and long-term program of expanding *all* categories of its military power . . . in technological quality and global reach."[2]

Outraged American public reaction to the Soviet invasion of Afghanistan, and the attention the public paid to the defense-preparedness issue in the 1980 election campaign, suggest that the American people may now be ready to make up for lost time, provided there were a working consensus on the measures possible and necessary to meet the challenge. There is not yet such a consensus. Besides, the historical record shows recurring ambiguities in the perceptions of both the American public and its leadership regarding the terms and requirements of the continuing U.S.-Soviet power competition. It was this ambivalence in American perceptions and faltering in American determination, over the past decade and a half, which enabled the Soviet Union to achieve overall strategic parity with the United States and, quite possibly, superiority in certain categories of both strategic and conventional weapons and forces.

Responsibility for the inadequate U.S. response to the sustained build-up of Soviet power cannot be fixed in partisan political terms. There is ample blame to be shared by at least four Administrations representing both parties, and by eight Democratic Congresses. The blame extends, also, to the generation of Americans, both youth and adults, who, during this period when the national will was being tested, displayed uncertainties of purpose and conflicting social and economic priorities that set political limits on U.S. defense strategy and spending.

The ill-starred, mismanaged, and ultimately humiliating national ordeal in Vietnam (during the Administrations of John F. Kennedy, Lyndon B. Johnson, and Richard M. Nixon) was the major contributing factor. Inability of the United States, despite overwhelming military power, to secure the right of self-determination for its South Vietnamese allies, in a decade of shared sacrifices, resulted in the diversion and wasting of incalculably valuable human, material, political, and moral resources. The experience resulted also in the erosion of confidence of a significant portion of the American public (and of foreign allies and friends) in the nation's international goals and strategies. Simultaneously, the American public's confidence in the competence of its national political and military leadership—and in the role of U.S. military power in global politics—was also gravely impaired.

The agonizing Vietnam experience helps explain the alacrity and then the euphoria with which political leadership and the American public, during the Johnson, Nixon, Ford, and early Carter Administrations, responded to Soviet proferring of détente. The bait was the prospect for reaching with the Soviet Union a string of agreements intended to ease tensions, reduce the risk of war, and normalize East-West cooperation. Areas for negotiation included nuclear nonproliferation, strategic arms limitations, mutual and balanced force reductions in Europe, and the expansion of East-West commercial, scientific, and cultural cooperation. Failure of a military solution in the conflict with Soviet-subsidized North Vietnam reinforced latent American yearnings for nonbellicose solutions to other problems on the agenda of the U.S.-Soviet competition.

It may be that these yearnings also confirmed the notorious brevity of attention span of a democratic people for protracted power contests, distant from immediate domestic concerns. Although the American people have time and again demonstrated their readiness to respond to a specific and clearly perceived foreign challenge, they have showed limited endurance in meeting the demands of a prolonged, ambiguous, and unlikely-to-be-decisive struggle such as the localized combat in Korea or Vietnam or the fatiguing global, ideological-military competition with the Soviet Union.

There has been, in addition, a long-persisting division of opinion among American and other Western politicians, academics, and editorialists, as well as laymen, regarding Soviet "intentions." The debate deals with such questions as whether Soviet aims are implacably hostile to the interests of the United States or whether Soviet leadership can be "converted"—out of self-interest, if not the mutual interest—to the acceptance of common and binding rules for peaceful competition within an increasingly structured and stable world order. In short, can the superpower struggle be shifted by mutual accommodation from the military to essentially nonmilitary arenas, and, if so, what U.S. policies and strategies would most likely contribute to this result? During the 1960s and most of the 1970s there was serious debate whether the United States should seek to maintain military superiority, should accept Soviet parity, or should make unilateral arms concessions to encourage reciprocal Soviet restraint.

America's defense policies and diplomacy have reflected the inconclusiveness of this debate in the periodic zigging and zagging of prominent sectors of domestic public opinion toward one point or another on this attitudinal compass. Unsurprisingly, given the nonexistent role of public debate in the Soviet Union, Soviet policy has been undeviating in the determination to achieve parity and then, from all evidence, superiority in critical areas of the power balance.

Fragmentation of American Politics

Other forces were at work in the 1960s and early 1970s which were in time to polarize—indeed, fragment—domestic American political cohesion, alter the nation's priorities, and undermine its capacity and political will to maintain a strategy and military posture necessary to keep a stable global power balance.

One such force has been the ascendancy of single-issue political causes, on top of already well-organized and abundantly financed traditional political interests and lobbies.

The heroic, nonviolent black struggle for equal rights gathered momentum under the Administrations of Harry S. Truman, Dwight D. Eisenhower, and Kennedy. Under the Johnson Administration it was raised to the level of a national crusade. By the late 1960s, as genuine progress was being made in dismantling institutionalized segregation and discrimination, the struggle shifted to highly controversial remedies for *de facto* discrimination and its consequences—mandating racial balance in ghettoized school systems, for example, and promoting affirmative action in educational and job opportunities. This latter stage of the prolonged struggle for actual racial equality has contributed to an ideological polarization of American politics, and continues to be waged in the courts and the political arena.

Prompted in part by early black political and judicial successes, a host of other "equal rights" interest groups have proliferated since the late 1960s—Native American, Hispanic, and other ethnic groups; the women's liberation movement, focusing on the Equal Rights Amendment and abortion by choice; gay liberation; and others. Each of these causes has generated its own passionate countermovement or political resistance, drawing new and bitter lines in national politics, and escalating the involvement in partisan politics of organized religion and ideological extremism of the right and left. Equally bitter political and ideological lines have been drawn on other single-issue causes such as environmental protection, consumerism, capital punishment, school prayer, registration of hand guns, nuclear-generated energy, and more.

The youth rebellion of the late 1960s had an extraordinarily unsettling impact on American politics that continues to be felt throughout the society. Although it was an international phenomenon of the time, its American manifestation took the form of a corrosive attack on established politics, institutions, and life styles. Fringe groups within the youth rebellion helped make demonstrations, sit-ins, teach-ins, boycotts, and street violence as much a part of the political scene as the more traditional channels of political expression through party organizations and the ballot box.

Much of the vehemence of American domestic politics in the late 1960s and early 1970s was fed by the organized opposition of young people and adults, including a coalition of single-issue movements and a growing number of liberal political leaders, to continued U.S. involvement in Vietnam. Indeed, Vietnam became the litmus of political polarization in that era, the common test distinguishing orthodoxy from protest, right from left, the "old" politics and morality from the "new."

Among the surviving effects of this fragmentation are renewed tensions in the division of power between the federal and state governments, "participatory" reforms in party-platform and nominating procedures (especially in the Democratic Party), the heavy turnover since 1968 in the membership of both the Senate and House, the breakdown of leadership authority and party discipline in both houses of Congress, and the rapid growth in numbers of voters who consider themselves "independents" at the expense of both parties. The traumatic political assassinations in 1968 of Senator Robert F. Kennedy and the Reverend Martin Luther King, Jr., and the prolonged unfolding of the 1972–74 Watergate-related scandals, served only to deepen the nation's political malaise and weaken its sense of political legitimacy. Throughout that era, various public-opinion polls showed declining public confidence in the leadership of virtually all American political and social institutions.

Finally, the intense fervor of the 1960s for domestic political and social reform, however pure the motives of the grass-roots activists and the elected leaders who responded to it, led to a skewing of national priorities and a straining of fiscal resources. In the increasingly antiwar climate, the preoccupation with domestic affairs insured that expenditures for national security would be assigned a declining priority through the decade of the 1970s.

The policy of containment of Soviet expansionism through military deterrence, which generally had the support of a bipartisan consensus from 1948 (year of the Soviet-backed coup in Czechoslovakia and the Berlin blockade and airlift) through the Korean War of 1950–53 and several brief détentes during the 1950s and 1960s, broke down during the conflict in Vietnam— the first war in history to be waged every evening in all its blood and horror on television in every American living room.

Ironically, the 1965–68 escalation of the U.S. military commitment to the survival of an independent South Vietnam— which initially had broad public and congressional support— was intended to produce an effect on the superpower competition opposite to the eventual outcome. U.S. intervention in Vietnam—as, a decade and a half earlier, in Korea[3]— was meant to demonstrate the power and will of the United States to contain communist expansionism, as represented in both of those wars by massive Soviet and Chinese arms and economic support of the Northern aggressors. Failure to prevent a total North Vietnamese victory (and eventual takeover of the rest of Indochina) presented the world with the contrary spectacle of a polarization of American domestic politics, a near paralysis of American will to engage in the risks of global power politics, and an American retreat from the strategy of containment.

Erosion of the Economic Base of Power

Among the heritages of the Kennedy, Johnson, and Nixon Administrations was a multiplying of social programs, income transfers, new regulatory regimes, and federal revenue-sharing schemes. They were intended to achieve such social goals as improving the incomes, nutrition, and health services available to the poorest members of the society; speeding the assimilation of the disadvantaged into the mainstream economy; cleaning up environmental pollution; reducing health and safety hazards; and a host of others, each supported by politically powerful constituencies and lobbies, in alliance with the federal bureau-cracies established to administer the programs. The policy test that no Administration or Congress has faced successfully from the mid-1960s to the present, is not whether society has the right to mandate such social goods (which of course it has), but rather what mix and scale of social consumption the society can *afford*, given competing priorities (such as national defense) and taking into account the capacity of the wealth-producing sectors of the society to generate enough surplus to pay for such legislated consumption.

Fiscal strains of this competition for public funds were reck-lessly compounded by the political decision of first the Johnson Administration and then Congress, in 1965–66, to delay until too late the tax increases needed to fight both the war in Vietnam and the domestic war on poverty. The record early-sixties price stability was shattered in the inflationary spiral which still persists. Moreover, the initial inflationary push was exacerbated successively by the Nixon Administration's domestic and international monetary policies (especially over-stimulation of the heated U.S. economy in the 1972 preelection period) and by the 1973–74 oil crisis and subsequent rounds of stiff price increases for OPEC oil.

Remedies have been slow in coming. No significant legislation was passed during either the Nixon or Ford Administration to promote energy conservation or new-energy development. After three years the Carter Administration succeeded in pushing various pieces of an energy program through a reluctant Congress, but the United States and its industrialized allies are expected to continue heavily dependent on imported oil well beyond the coming decade. However, partly because of higher gasoline prices, the American people have reduced significantly their consumption of gasoline during the past two years, permitting a corresponding reduction in oil imports.

It is also only in the last two years that political, business, and academic leadership—with considerable support from the communications media—have paid serious and sustained attention to the structural distortions in the American economy resulting from chronic inflation, tax and other disincentives to savings and investment, and faulty investment and marketing decisions by U.S. industrial management. Among the most serious of these distortions are lagging capital investment in domestic U.S. plant and equipment, increasing obsolescence of manufacturing capacity, slowing down of the rate of product innovation, flattening of productivity gains in many manufacturing industries, and deterioration of U.S. international competitiveness in important industrial sectors, such as steel, automobiles, and consumer electronics.[4]

Erosion of the economic base of American power has contributed throughout the 1970s to chronic inflation, high unemployment, and insufficient economic growth to support adequately both domestic and foreign priorities. At this late stage in the process of deterioration, it means limited capacity and flexibility to undertake a large-scale and rapid defense build-up. Effects of past political constraints on defense spending are now being reinforced by both fiscal constraints in anti-inflationary federal budgeting and actual physical limits in the capacity and quality of the nation's industrial base.

Beginning the U.S. Defense Build-Down

Despite ample evidence of the Soviet Union's determination to overtake the United States in *politically usable* military power (and thus never again to have to back down in a direct U.S.-Soviet confrontation, as it had to do in Cuba), the United States acquiesced in what has proved to be a threat to the strategic power balance. It did so tacitly in the mid-to-late 1960s (Johnson Administration) by imposing unilateral limits on the deployment of U.S. strategic weapons, while ultimately pouring $30 billion into an unwinnable military effort in Vietnam. The acquiescence was explicit in the Nixon Administration.

Annual percentage increases in budget outlays of 19.8 percent in 1967 and 15.4 percent in 1968 expressed last gasp efforts of the Johnson Administration to apply increased military pressure to move the Vietnam conflict from the battlefield to the conference table. Throughout the late 1960s and early 1970s, however, defense procurement was heavily concentrated on Vietnam requirements. During those years the United States neglected to match the ongoing Soviet build-up in strategic nuclear weapons and blue-water naval power, and mounting

Soviet threats in other theaters more directly threatening to U.S. interests, especially Europe.

In 1968 the Johnson Administration, then in its final year, called a halt to any further build-up of the domestically divisive U.S. military commitment in Vietnam. Quickly recovering from the shock of the Soviet-Warsaw Pact military intervention in Czechoslovakia that spring, Johnson sought a summit with the Soviet Union to explore reciprocal limits on strategic arms and Soviet assistance in obtaining a negotiated settlement in Vietnam. Neither materialized. Soon after the Nixon Administration took office in January 1969, both avenues were reopened. The era of détente was launched, and wide-ranging negotiations were begun on trade, cultural, and other channels for expanded U.S.-Soviet cooperation. However, the Soviet Union provided no perceptible help for a negotiated Vietnam peace, as the Nixon Administration set about fulfilling its campaign pledge to end the war, which it did four years later.

Throughout the first Nixon term, 1969–72, public and congressional opposition to the war and defense spending was at a peak. According to a July 1969 Gallup public-opinion survey, 52 percent of all American adults felt that current defense spending was "too much," 8 percent felt it was "too little," and 31 percent felt it was "about right." In May 1971 Senate Majority Leader Mike Mansfield proposed an amendment to the Draft Extension Law which would have required cutting U.S. forces in Europe by half.[5]

In this climate, defense outlays during the six Nixon years were flattened to annual increases of .9 percent in 1969, –1.0 percent in 1970, –3.6 percent in 1971, 1.1 percent in 1972, –2.7 percent in 1973, and 4.4 percent in 1974. Taking account of inflation, defense outlays actually declined in each of those six years.

Although Administration defense-budget requests were higher than Congress would accept, the strategic doctrines of the Nixon Administration were consistent with restraint in defense spending. For example, the Administration explicitly articulated for the first time the principle of parity with (rather than superiority over) the Soviet Union. This shift assumed that a stable power balance based on "mutually assured destruction" could be maintained by (1) a "strategic sufficiency" in U.S. arms levels (taking account of U.S. technological superiority, including weapons accuracy) and (2) "linkage diplomacy." Through this new diplomacy, the United States and the Soviet Union were expected to find common interest in constructing the foundations of "a generation of peace" by "avoiding a nuclear confrontation," reducing "the enormous cost of arms," increasing "trade and contact between us," and giving "our competition a creative direction" by jointly meeting "the global challenge of economic and social development."[6]

Détente and the Guam Doctrine

In its four-year effort to extricate U.S. forces from Vietnam with minimum damage to the national interest and honor, or to the survivability of its South Vietnamese ally, the Nixon Administration faced an adversary, North Vietnam, that was unwilling to negotiate a compromise peace. Instead, the North was determined to wait out the inevitable U.S. withdrawal and then take its chances on total victory over the South. A second adversary, the Soviet Union, provided no help toward a negotiated peace, but continued its vast military aid to North Vietnam and its own steady arms build-up, while disarmingly inviting other forms of U.S.-Soviet "cooperation" through détente. Finally, there was mounting U.S. public and congressional opposition to the dragging out of the war, and growing enthusiasm for détente.

The Administration's strategy, as enunciated by President Nixon and National Security Assistant (later Secretary of State) Kissinger was, over the short run, to escalate the bombing and other military pressures on North Vietnam, while continuing to press the Soviet Union for meaningful help in obtaining a negotiated peace and honorable U.S. withdrawal from Vietnam. Over the longer run, the strategy was to offer the communist powers incentives and disincentives for the observance of rules leading to "a new and stable framework of international relationships," to be "cemented by the shared goal of coexistence and the shared practice of accommodation."[7]

The Administration considered the key to this "new American role" in the world to be the Guam (or Nixon) Doctrine, pronounced in the summer of 1969 and later elaborated. The doctrine represented a retrenchment from the open-ended commitment of the 1947 Truman Doctrine that "it must be the policy of the United States to support free peoples who are resisting subjugation by armed minorities or by outside pressures." The retrenchment reflected, however, profound changes that had taken place in the interim, including the loss of U.S. nuclear monopoly, European and Japanese economic recovery, establishment of NATO, narrowing of the power gap between the United States and the Soviet Union, and the Vietnam experience and accompanying domestic political and budgetary constraints on engagement of U.S. military power. The Guam Doctrine comprised three elements:

1. "The United States will keep all its treaty commitments."
2. "We shall provide a shield if a nuclear power threatens the freedom of a nation allied with us or of a nation whose survival we consider vital to our security."

3. "In cases involving other types of aggression we shall furnish military and economic assistance when requested in accordance with our treaty commitments. But we shall look to the nation directly threatened to assume the primary responsibility of providing the manpower for its defense."[8]

In defense policy, the Guam Doctrine lent justification to the concept of "strategic sufficiency" (as distinguished from "superiority"), which President Nixon defined as (1) "enough force to inflict a level of damage on a potential aggressor sufficient to deter him from attacking" and (2) "maintenance of forces adequate to prevent us and our allies from being coerced."[9] Implementation of the new policy entailed a scaling down of the Johnson Administration's "two-and-a-half war" strategy (theoretical U.S. capacity to wage simultaneous major wars in Europe *and* Asia, plus a minor regional conflict elsewhere) to a "one-and-a-half war" strategy (Europe *or* Asia, plus a regional contingency).[10]

Accordingly, beginning in 1969, the Administration announced U.S. military force reductions of 20,000 in South Korea, 12,000 in Japan, 5,000 in Okinawa, 16,000 in Thailand, and 9,000 in the Philippines, plus a reduction of 86,000 in U.S. Government personnel stationed abroad. (The foreign aid budget was increased by $1 billion, however, in recognition that the Guam Doctrine implied increased aid to allies.)

The Guam Doctrine also provided a basis, beginning in 1971, for surrogating to the Shah of Iran primary police-power responsibility for maintaining peace in the Persian Gulf area, and for selling the Shah billions in sophisticated American arms between 1971 and his overthrow in early 1979.

On July 1, 1973, the Nixon Admnistration ended the military draft. Stand-by registration for the draft was abandoned in 1975, by the Ford Administration.

Détente Replaces Containment

The Nixon Administration was no more successful than its predecessor in obtaining a negotiated settlement that would reasonably allow for the survival of an independent South Vietnam—or even an independent Laos or Cambodia. Nor can the final U.S. withdrawal and subsequent South Vietnamese collapse be portrayed as anything other than a defeat for the United States.

Nonetheless, progress on détente with the Soviet Union and, more appropriately, the 1972 opening to China were presented to the American people as historic "breakthroughs." Even the narrowing of the U.S.-Soviet power gap presented an opportunity: "The more nearly equal strategic balance between the United States and the Soviet Union suggested that conditions might be optimal for reaching agreement to limit strategic competition."[11] At the 1972 Moscow summit, as the president later reported to Congress, the United States and the Soviet Unon had "agreed on basic principles to govern our relations," an achievement he described as a "major movement toward a steadier and more conservative relationship." He acknowledged, however, that "areas of tension and potential conflict remain and certain patterns of Soviet behavior continue to cause concern."[12]

Yet the Administration felt some ambivalence about its pursuit of détente. Kissinger recalls that his motives were partly tactical—"to maximize Soviet dilemmas and reduce Soviet influence as in the Middle East"—and partly domestic—"to outmaneuver the 'peace' pressures so we could rally our public if a showdown proved inevitable." He also acknowledges his "conviction that the moral imperative of leadership in our time was to keep open the prospect, however slim, of a fundamental change, of doing our utmost so that Armageddon did not descend on us through neglect or lack of foresight." The quest for peaceful coexistence "might sap our vigilance," but "a crusading policy of confrontation" would not necessarily succeed, and "would risk our national cohesion and our alliances."[13]

For President Nixon, the principal fruit of détente was the SALT I treaty, signed in Moscow in the spring of 1972, fourth in a series of arms-control agreements negotiated with the Soviet Union by the Nixon Administration. SALT I limited both countries' deployment of antiballistic missiles (ABMs) and legitimated Soviet numerical superiority in land-based intercontinental ballistic missiles (ICBMs) and sea-launched missiles (SLBMs), on the presumption that a more equitable balance could be negotiated in SALT II. By that time the United States was expected to have under advanced development the B-1 bomber, the Trident nuclear-powered missile submarine, and some form of the MX mobile missile. The combination of these weapons developments was intended to insure, in case of a Soviet first strike, the survival of an overwhelming—and credible—U.S. retaliatory capacity.[14]

Meanwhile, what Nixon had called the disturbing "patterns of Soviet behavior" continued. The Soviet Union rapidly deployed a superior counterforce capability—missiles with the power and accuracy to destroy in a preemptive strike a high percentage of the frozen U.S. inventory of retaliatory missiles. In 1973 the Soviet Union played the role of *provocateur* in preparations for the surprise Yom Kippur-Ramadan war, providing combat-support military advisers as well as vast amounts of arms to Egypt and Syria. Massive airlifts of arms from U.S. arsenals were required to insure Israel's survival. Then Washington had to issue a virtual ultimatum when Moscow threatened to airlift Soviet troops into the area to prevent a total Egyptian defeat. (Even so, the Nixon Administration later invited the Soviet Union to participate in guaranteeing the cease-fire.)

After Vietnam, Watergate

U.S. involvement in Vietnam ended with the withdrawal of the last American troops on March 29, 1973, two months after the signing in Paris of the cease-fire agreement. Despite the frustrations of four years of negotiations in which the North Vietnamese made not a single substantive concession, and the Soviet Union continued to provide unstinting support to Hanoi's military forces, even as they widened the war into Laos and Cambodia, Kissinger had hopes that the cease-fire would hold and that détente would help.

He believed that the agreement was workable because it "reflected a true equilibrium of forces on the ground," because "Saigon was strong enough to deal with . . . low-level violations," and because "the implicit threat of our retaliation would be likely to deter massive violations." Kissinger also hoped that the postwar U.S. aid promised by both Johnson and Nixon to *all* Indochina "might possibly even turn Hanoi's attention (and manpower) to tasks of construction if the new realities took hold for a sufficient period of time." Furthermore, "we would use our new relationships with Moscow and Peking to foster restraint."[15]

The agreement did not work. Neither Moscow nor Peking exercised any effective restraint in Hanoi, and the Nixon Administration lacked the domestic political authority to enforce the agreement. Congress refused to authorize the $750 million in supplementary aid to South Vietnam that Nixon requested. In the spring of 1975 South Vietnamese resistance collapsed, and Saigon capitulated to fourteen Soviet-equipped North Vietnamese divisions.

In due course, with continuing Soviet (but diminishing Chinese) support, Hanoi extended its effective military and political control over Laos, installed two successive governments in Cambodia, and now controls virtually all the surviving populations of both countries. Hanoi has also since entered into formal alliance with Moscow, providing the Soviet navy with access to Haiphong harbor and to the extensive and intact U.S.-built port facilities at Cam Ranh Bay and Da Nang.

By the summer of 1973, in any event, the Nixon Administration itself was under siege of investigative reporters, the Senate select committee, and the courts, as Watergate and related scandals unraveled. In the midst of the 1973 Middle East crisis (when the Nixon Administration's all-out support for beleaguered Israel triggered the Arab oil embargo and continuing Arab use of the "oil weapon"), Vice President Spiro Agnew was forced to resign under uncontested criminal charges. Within less than a year—on August 9, 1974—President Nixon was also forced out of office, under threat of impeachment. Throughout that harrowing period, as the powers of executive leadership steadily hemorrhaged, the execution of U.S. foreign and defense polices relied almost entirely on momentum.

Picking Up the Pieces

Collapse of American policy in Southeast Asia and the discrediting and forced resignation of a president greatly compounded the problems of the unelected Ford Administration in conducting a coherent foreign policy, credible to both allies and adversaries. Senator George S. McGovern's neo-isolationist

"Come home, America" theme of the 1972 presidential campaign had been thoroughly repudiated at the polls, but the strategy of waging the superpower competition by maintaining—and being willing to employ—U.S. military power and power-based diplomacy had been badly discredited in Vietnam.

The dominant political mood in Congress, including most of the liberal Democratic leadership and a group of Republican liberals, favored a continuing decline in defense spending and increased reliance on détente, which was perceived as a substitute or successor to cold war. Among foreign-policy conservatives of both parties, including much of the Republican leadership and Democratic defense specialists, détente was highly suspect precisely because of the fear that reliance on it would sap the nation's will and deplete the military strength necessary to contain Soviet expansionism.

This controversy persuaded President Ford to drop the word détente from the Administration's vocabulary during his 1976 battle with Governor Ronald Reagan for the Republican nomination. Without abandoning the pursuit of negotiated cooperation with the Soviet Union, Ford pressed for a reversal of the six-year decline in defense outlays, arguing in his State of the Union message to Congress on January 19, 1976:

A strong defense posture gives weight to our values and our views in international negotiations; it assures the vigor of our alliances; and it sustains our efforts to promote settlements of international conflicts. Only from a position of strength can we negotiate a balanced agreement to limit the growth of nuclear arms. Only a balanced agreement will serve our interest and minimize the threat of nuclear confrontation.

Budgeted defense outlays were increased a nominal 9.5 percent in 1975, 4.6 percent in 1976, and 9.1 percent in 1977, despite public and congressional resistance,[16] the 1974–75 recession (the worst in four decades), and a raging 12 percent inflation (cut in half by the beginning of 1976, primarily as a result of the recession).

The Ford Administration inherited other pernicious problems. Congressional and popular rebellion against the "imperial presidencies" (of Johnson and Nixon in particular) found expression in the War Powers Act of 1973, which sharply curtailed the authority of the president as commander in chief. Leaks and Watergate revelations, along with documents obtained by scholars and journalists under the Freedom of Information Act, exposed excesses and illegalities commited by intelligence agencies. This led to efforts (so far unsuccessful) to reform and monitor these agencies, treating them as ordinary service bureaucracies, rather than vital and necessarily covert instruments of national security.[17]

The greatest disappointment to the Ford Administration was its inability to persuade Congress to support U.S. aid, either covert or through open military deliveries, to moderate Angolan political forces resisting the powerful intervention of Soviet-ferried Cuban military units fighting on the side of local Marxists.

On détente, the Administration made substantial progress toward a SALT II treaty at the November 1974 Vladivostok summit, and it continued the normalization of relations with China at a cautious pace. But only one major détente agreement was signed. This was the 1975 Helsinki Accords (Final Act of the Conference on Security and Cooperation in Europe, or CSCE), which outlawed any alteration by force of postwar European boundaries and, inferentially, acknowledged Soviet hegemony in Eastern Europe, in exchange for Soviet commitments to the expansion of commercial, cultural, and other peaceful cooperation with the West, and to the mutual observance, under mutual scrutiny, of human rights.

With the changing of Administrations in January 1977, the national ambivalence persisted on the question whether détente was a substitute for or an instrument of cold-war politics, and whether America's defense posture was excessive, adequate, or woefully inadequate to the challenges the nation would face.

Notes

1. Theoretically, the revised "countervailing" nuclear-targeting strategy acknowledged by the Carter Administration in August 1980 would provide the president with more flexible options in responding, for example, to a Soviet military thrust to seal the Gulf. He could order pinpointed nuclear strikes against selected Soviet targets, such as missile silos, or even against military or political command centers, instead of resorting to all-out nuclear attack against Soviet population centers, as envisaged under the previous doctrine of "mutually assured destruction" (or MAD), that both sides have tacitly accepted since the mid-1960s. Yet the Pentagon is not confident that a countervailing strategy could be kept from escalating to full-scale war. This dilemma undermines the credibility of a flexible targeting strategy as a deterrent.

2. Henry A. Kissinger, *The White House Years* (Boston: Little, Brown and Company, 1979), pp. 196–97.

3. Public opposition to the "limited war" in Korea also grew in proportion to the ambiguity of UN objectives and the impossibility of decisive "victory." Revulsion against the war was a major factor in the 1952 presidential elections but did not reach the proportions of the popular protest against the Vietnam conflict.

4. U.S. share of the industrialized world's earnings from exports of manufactured goods declined from 22.4 percent in 1960 to 17.4 percent in 1979. The trend reflects both dollar depreciation and inflation, as

well as declining competitiveness—in both domestic and foreign markets—of key U.S. manufacturing industries. Other U.S. industries —textiles, machinery, computers and chemicals, for example—and technology-intensive U.S. agriculture continue to be highly competitive internationally and domestically.

5. This proposal was defeated by marshaling testimony from the old, bipartisan "foreign-policy establishment," led by former Secretary of State Dean Acheson, and by alarmed reactions from NATO allies and an unexpected Soviet offer to open negotiations on mutual troop reductions in Europe.

6. President Richard M. Nixon, in an address to the United Nations, October 23, 1970.

7. Richard Nixon, *U.S. Foreign Policy for the 1970's, Building for Peace—A Report to the Congress, February 25, 1971* (Washington, D.C.: U.S. Government Printing Office), p. 170. In *The White House Years*, Kissinger asserts that Nixon and he accepted "the principle of détente," despite their shared skepticism, at the strong urging of European allies and out of fears that "if America was intransigent, we risked being isolated within the alliance and pushing Europe toward neutralism" (p. 403). A similar rationale was undoubtedly applicable to American public and congressional attitudes.

8. Nixon, *A Report to the Congress, February 25, 1971*, pp. 12–14. These principles had been anticipated in Nixon's article, "Asia After Viet Nam," *Foreign Affairs*, October 1967, p. 111–125, in which he called for "(a) a collective effort by the nations of [a less stable] region to contain [a communist] threat by themselves; and, if that effort fails, (b) a collective request to the United States for assistance."

9. Nixon, *A Report to the Congress, February 25, 1971*, p. 170.

10. The Soviet Union, with forty-six divisions on the China front, thirty in Eastern Europe, and thirty-five in the western Soviet Union, plus its forces now fighting in Afghanistan, may be said to possess at least a "two-and-a-half war" capability.

11. Richard Nixon, *U.S. Foreign Policy for the 1970's, Shaping a Durable Peace—A Report to the Congress, May 3, 1973* (Washington, D.C.: U.S. Government Printing Office), p. 27.

12. *Ibid.,* p. 11.

13. Kissinger, *The White House Years*, pp. 1255–56.

14. Development of all three systems was delayed by controversy among experts and technical problems, as well as political resistance and limited funding. In 1977 the Carter Administration canceled the B-1 bomber and slowed the MX and Trident programs. During 1979 the MX was reinstated, the first Trident submarine was launched two years behind schedule, and construction of an additional six boats was accelerated. However, controversy continues over the design and even utility of the MX layout, and the Trident program has serious technical and managerial problems and cost overruns.

15. Kissinger, *The White House Years*, p. 1470.

16. In September 1974 the Gallup Organization reported that 44 percent of the American public still considered current defense spending "too much," while only 12 percent considered it "too little."

17. No arm of the U.S. Government can be permitted to be a law unto itself or to flout the constitutional rights of citizens. Judicial as well as congressional oversight of domestic intelligence and counter-intelligence activities involving American citizens, as provided in existing law, is proper and necessary. Yet, as in war, so also in the grim gray area of near war, the gathering of critical intelligence and the protecting of vital political and technological secrets is a necessary—and necessarily secret—professionalized responsibility. The more difficult and yet unresolved question is how to prevent, without compromising proper secrecy and professionalism, covert actions overseas which violate American standards of morality or undermine declared U.S. political objectives.

III   Reversing the Defense Build-Down

In his final defense budget, President Ford called for the first real increase in defense spending since 1968. In his unsuccessful reelection campaign of 1976, he urged a sustained defense build-up and (while avoiding the term détente) continuation of the SALT process. The Carter Administration entered office the following January, pledged to cut $5–7 billion ("fat, not muscle") from the defense budget, to continue the phased withdrawal of U.S. ground forces from South Korea, to reduce U.S. arms sales abroad, and (as the president put it in his May 22, 1977, commencement address at Notre Dame), "to engage the Soviet Union in a joint effort to halt the strategic arms race"—that is, to continue the negotiations leading to a SALT II treaty.[1]

Each of these Carter pledges was later reversed or stillborn.

Cuts in the defense budget were delayed and then abandoned in the course of a review of defense requirements and growing apprehension about the Soviet arms build-up. Troop withdrawals from South Korea were halted following intelligence reassessment of the balance of forces on the peninsula and political reappraisal of the probable damage any further weakening of the U.S. military presence in the Western Pacific would have on the credibility of U.S. commitments to its Pacific-Asian allies, notably Japan, South Korea, and the Philippines. U.S. arms sales, in the Middle East in particular, continued in the absence of restraint on the part of the Soviet Union or NATO allies. After a false start, when the USSR flatly rejected U.S. proposals for deep reciprocal cuts in offensive weapons, a more limited SALT II treaty was signed on June 18, 1979. It quickly ran into bipartisan resistance in the Senate, however, on grounds that the treaty limits on arms were either insufficient or disadvantageous to the United States, or were not adequately verifiable. Administration efforts to win support of two thirds of the Senate for ratification were suspended following the invasion of Afghanistan.

On defense procurement and spending, the Carter Administration wavered and waffled, but the net result was to reverse the downward trend. The controversial B-1 bomber program was canceled, but the Administration accelerated the development of the cruise missile, which it considered a more cost-effective weapon. The production schedule for the Trident nuclear submarine was slowed for technical and budgetary reasons, but then accelerated in 1979, as were other naval shipbuilding programs.

In the summer of 1979 (prior to the invasion of Afghanistan) the Administration initiated a Pentagon study of available options for rapidly upgrading U.S. strategic capabilities. In this context, Carter ordered the resumption of the MX mobile-missile program and the development of rapid-deployment forces.

The MX issue demonstrates the complexity of the continuing debate regarding the mix of strategic weapons appropriate for both the short term and the late 1980s and the 1990s. The MX as now conceived is a mobile missile that can be sped by rail from one to another of a number of covered launching chambers, in a kind of "shell game." Periodically all the chambers would be uncovered to permit Soviet satellites to verify that there is only one missile on each track. Purpose of the MX is to overcome the vulnerability of existing U.S. land-based missiles, which are in fixed silos and might be knocked out in a preemptive strike by more numerous, more powerful, and increasingly accurate Soviet ICBMs.

Carter had slowed the MX development program in 1977 on grounds of cost, the long lead time required, uncertainties about the efficacy of the weapon, and environmentalist opposition. He reinstated the program in 1979, in part at least to win Senate votes for the SALT II treaty. Linkage to the treaty made theoretical sense because the treaty would have limited the number of Soviet (as well as American) ICBMs and the number of MIRVed warheads permitted on each ICBM. Since the MX system would present the Soviet Union with many more potential targets (4,600 under current plans) than the number of warheads that country would be permitted, the survivability of U.S. land-based missiles (and therefore the credibility of the U.S. deterrent) would be greatly improved. Without the SALT II ceilings, however, there would be no restraint on the number of missiles and warheads that the USSR might target against U.S. land-based missiles. According to one recent U.S. intelligence estimate, for example, by 1985—when the MX system could be deployed—the Soviet Union could acquire a missile arsenal of 16,000 nuclear warheads, or about twice the number of land- and sea-based missiles the United States plans to have at that time. The MX, in other words, without new SALT limits, could become vulnerable to a Soviet first strike even before the system is deployed.[2]

The Reagan Administration is committed in principle to higher increases in defense spending than those projected by its predecessor, and to early resumption of the SALT process, in the hopes of negotiating a better treaty than the "flawed" SALT II. It remains problematical whether the U.S. strategic deterrent will be less vulnerable and more credible by the mid-1980s than it is today. Indeed, without the restraints of new SALT agreements, and in the absence of a rapid build-up of U.S. strategic power, it is conceivable that the current eight-to-six U.S. numerical advantage in warheads, and superiority in weapons accuracy, will soon vanish.

Soviet attainment of clear-cut strategic superiority over the United States would not automatically confirm a Soviet doctrine that nuclear war is feasible and winnable. It would, however, impose practical limits on the political uses of U.S. military power, while correspondingly easing the restraints on Soviet military adventurism. Demonstrable U.S. strategic inferiority would also imply a rapid decline in U.S. influence throughout the developing world and erosion of American usefulness as a friend and reliable ally.

A genuine national debate has barely begun on the strategies to overcome actual or anticipated vulnerabilities in U.S. defense posture. The 1980 campaign debates dealt largely in symbolic generalities such as the relative leadership capabilities of the candidates in maintaining peace or "standing up to the Russians," and disagreements over the merits of the SALT II treaty. Little or no attention was addressed to such fundamental questions as: What types of direct and indirect military challenges must the United States be prepared to meet through the balance of this decade? What mix of forces and weapons—conventional as well as strategic—will, in the face of these possible challenges, enable the United States to insure its own security, and that of its allies and friends, and to protect their collective vital interests around the globe? Given the present state of American defenses, and weaknesses in the American economy and industrial plant, what are the most cost-effective means for achieving optimum national security during the period of greatest U.S. vulnerability? What proportion of increased defense spending should go into research and development, new hardware, and improved maintenance, and what proportion into recruiting, training, and retaining needed manpower levels? And can manpower needs be realized without reinstituting the draft?

These are not questions of "fact," which can be answered unequivocally by technical experts, nor are they questions which yield to slogans symbolizing political intent. These are political questions in the fullest sense of the term. Answers will flow only from extended and informed public debate, leading to a more coherent political consensus on the nature of the challenges the nation faces and on America's purposes, priorities, and means in responding to those challenges. A working bipartisan consensus on realistic American strategies for the 1980s is the essential prior step to building up the military requirements for carrying out those strategies.[3]

It would be wholly unrealistic for the United States to attempt to recover its earlier margin of overall strategic superiority or to attempt to create, equip, and deploy the massive conventional forces that would be required to expel the Soviet Union from Afghanistan and neutralize Soviet power around its perimeter. Yet it is surely within reach of the United States and its allies to build the combination of strategic and conventional power—including theater forces in Europe and the Middle East, and mobile forces that could be rapidly deployed into other crisis areas—that will raise prohibitively the risks and costs to the Soviet Union of continuing its present policies of expansionism.

An early test of leadership of the Reagan Administration will be its skill in building the understanding and support of the American people—and of America's allies and friends—for such a strategy. It is a crucial test since, in the final analysis, the 1980 election hinged on the question of effective presidential leadership.

Notes

1. Negotiations on strategic arms limitations were originally proposed by the Pentagon in 1966, as a means of slowing the arms race and stabilizing the strategic power balance. Although President Johnson was committed to the concept, negotiations leading to the SALT I treaty did not get under way until 1969, under President Nixon. That treaty placed mutually verifiable ceilings on both ICBMs and ABMs. The SALT process, which calls for a progression of reciprocal and verifiable agreements on arms limits, presumes that the essential framework for a stable power balance is a negotiated structure of *strategic parity*.

2. A less costly and quicker-to-install alternative to the MX has been under study: conversion of the smaller Minuteman III into a mobile weapon which could also be shuttled among shelters, by truck instead of rail, in existing Minuteman fields. Modification could be accomplished in as little as two years, improving the survivability of U.S. land-based missiles without posing for the Soviet Union the first-strike threat implied by the heavier, more accurate MX.

3. Late in the 1980 election campaign, a New York *Times*/CBS News poll reported that 56 percent of the respondents favored U.S. military superiority over the Soviet Union, 35 percent favored parity, and 5 percent would accept less than arms equality.

IV   Leadership and Followership

EACH OF the last four American presidents was frustrated, and his power eroded, by public disaffection with his foreign-policy leadership—Johnson and Nixon by growing opposition to the Vietnam War, and Ford—and especially Carter—by the deepening division over the promises and the pitfalls of détente. The gap between leadership and followership was reflected in Congress, where cuts in presidential defense-budget requests totaled $50 billion between 1968 and 1980. (The final Carter budget, however, was increased over Administration requests.)

The Carter Administration has been charged with weak leadership, and lagging behind Congress and the public. Carter, it is said, entered office with a naïve perception of the superpower competition, not recognizing until Afghanistan the nature of the long-term Soviet threat.[1] Hence, it is argued, the United States lost a priceless three years when it should have been regirding itself to cope with the Soviet challenges it now faces in the Gulf and around the world. The most-often cited example of Carter's naïveté is his "we are now free of that inordinate fear of communism" commencement address at Notre Dame University, five months into office on May 22, 1977. Rarely, however, is the statement recalled in context:

49

Being confident of our own future, we are now free of that inordinate fear of communism which once led us to embrace any dictator who joined in our fear. . . . We fought fire with fire, never thinking that fire is better fought with water. This approach failed, with Vietnam the best example of its intellectual and moral poverty. . . . Based on a strong defense capability, our policy must . . . seek to improve relations with the Soviet Union and with China in ways that are both more comprehensive and more reciprocal. Even if we cannot heal ideological divisions, we must reach accommodations that reduce the risk of war.

Even in context, Carter's guarded optimism seems somewhat outdated in the post-Afghanistan period. It hardly seemed so at the time, however, when a substantial majority of American public opinion supported a national strategy based on both détente and what was presumed to be prudent defense policies.[2] Indeed, Carter's May 1977 rhetoric echoed in many respects Nixon's rhetoric of almost exactly four years earlier, celebrating the achievements of his first Administration:

[Previously] our relations with the Soviet Union, and international relations generally, were still dominated by the fears, anxieties and atmosphere of the cold war. . . . Yet, beneath the surface . . . , world politics was in the process of a major transformation. . . . [Our goal is] to create mutual interest [with the Soviet Union] in maintaining and developing an international structure based on self-restraint in the pursuit of national interests.[3]

The 1979 Cuban "crisis" is offered as another example of Carter's indecisiveness as a leader. The suddenly discovered presence in Cuba of a Soviet brigade was at first declared "unacceptable" by Secretary of State Cyrus Vance, but later accepted on the basis of Soviet assurances that the unit did not and would not pose any threat to the United States. How one Soviet infantry brigade in Cuba threatens U.S. security has yet to be made clear; the more likely reason for the unit's presence is to shore up the internal security of the Castro regime, or train Cuban expeditionary forces, or both. (The issue of Soviet cheating on the 1962 understanding, reached after the missile crisis, about the presence of Soviet combat forces in Cuba remains a legitimate but still unanswered concern, however.) In any event, the passivity with which the Carter Administration responded to Cuba, and to Soviet, Cuban, and East German military involvement in civil wars in Angola, Ethiopia, Namibia, Zimbabwe, and the Yemens, sent signals, some have argued, of U.S. paralysis to the Soviet Union, and thus reassured the Kremlin that its intervention in Afghanistan would be cost-free.

Whatever the clarity of hindsight, especially in the aftermath of a sea of change in U.S. public opinion such as appears to have occurred during 1980, it is fair to question whether the Carter Administration—even if it had set out to do so—could have accomplished earlier, by more alarmed leadership, the same turnaround in public and congressional attitudes that the shock of Afghanistan accomplished. Until the threat to the West's energy security was made explicit by that invasion, and by the almost simultaneous taking of the hostages in Iran, it is uncertain whether a congressional majority and a preponderance of the American public could have been persuaded to abandon the post-Vietnam, "generation of peace" euphoria of détente, and to accept the costs of a faster defense build-up and a tougher U.S. negotiating stance vis-à-vis the Soviet Union. Certainly there has long been a hard core of bipartisan support for such a shift, in Congress and in public-opinion leadership. Yet, as the leadership records of the three previous presidents—Johnson, Nixon, and Ford—demonstrated, the limits on the realigning of national strategies are set by how far, how fast, and in what directions the nation is ready to follow.

Certainly the Reagan Administration has a freer hand than its predecessor to lead the country in new direction, but it does not have carte blanche. Wounds of self-doubt incurred in Vietnam have much healed, but the scars continue to bind. Ambivalences about American purposes and Soviet intentions in the world are less debilitating than they were before Afghanistan and Poland, but the United States has neither sufficient military-industrial superiority, nor, as yet, the national political cohesion (let alone the congeries of co-committed allies and reliable friends), to lead a 1950s-like global crusade against communism. A national consensus in support of an accelerated U.S. defense build-up no doubt now exists, but holding that consensus together will require a spelling out of national strategies and defense priorities that are perceived by the American people to be rational and necessary, as well as compatible with other high-priority economic and social demands on the government.

The task of presidential leadership is in large measure a task of educating, mobilizing, and holding public followership. What, for example, is it politically feasible for the chief executive to extract from Congress at a particular moment to provide teeth for America's power competition with the Soviet Union? The competing priorities in Congress, the bureaucracy, and organized public interests for nonmilitary-spending purposes, and for tax relief and counterinflationary budget balancing, must be considered. In addition to balancing these interests, the president must consider the lingering attachment of substantial sectors of American opinion to strategies based, not solely on power competition, but also on active superpower diplomacy, or what remains of détente.

Problems of followership also apply to American leadership of the alliance of democracies. In NATO, more than within the United States, ambivalence persists over how much of détente can be salvaged, and to what extent "normal" relations with the Soviet Union can and should be pursued, even as the alliance—meaning especially the United States—strengthens its capacity to compete ideologically, economically, and militarily with the Soviet Union.

No doubt an armed Soviet intervention in Poland, to suppress the independent unions' challenge to communist-party monopoly of political power, would quickly deflate surviving sentiments for détente in both the United States and Western Europe. The just-as-likely prospect that the Polish workers movement will be gradually suffocated domestically, under pressure of Soviet intimidation short of invasion, would probably have a less enduring impact on pro-détente leanings, especially in Europe.

Leading the Alliance

Complaints that the alliance of Atlantic and Pacific democracies is in "disarray" tend to overlook the fact that the alliance has seldom been in perfect "array"—at least not since the early postwar, cold-war years. At that time, the recovery of Western Europe and Japan depended on enlightened U.S. aid and trade policies, and the survival of the allies as independent political democracies rested even more palpably on U.S. mutual-security guarantees.

That era is gone. The major allies have earned equality in interests if not in GNP, and in fact are rapidly approaching the United States in per capita GNP. The United States continues to be paramount in power within the alliance, with proportionately greater obligations on behalf of the alliance. Yet it cannot simply command automatic conformity of its allies to U.S. policies. NATO, ANZUS (Tripartite Security Treaty linking Australia, New Zealand, and the United States), and the U.S.-Japan Security Treaty are not the Warsaw Pact, nor are America's allies satellites in fact or inclination.

Much of the alliance disarray during the 1970s was due to erratic and often unpredictable U.S. unilateralism in economic and monetary as well as political and military policies. Following the U.S. withdrawal from Vietnam and the reduction of U.S. military forces abroad, there was also growing allied unease about the attrition of U.S. military supremacy, and an erosion of confidence in the firmness of the American public's commitment (and Congress's) to collective security.

It is ironical that, although much of the impetus for the 1970s détente came from Western Europe, the eagerness with which the United States embraced that détente raised European fears of a bipolar U.S.-Soviet "directorate," ready to dispose of global issues without proper attention to allied interests. Suspension of détente diplomacy (whether brief or prolonged) raises different allied fears of an unrestrained and increasingly dangerous arms race, loss of lucrative markets in East-West trade, and a breakdown of the East-West communications necessary to prevent deepening hostility—and even war, through miscalculation or accident.

What has been missing in alliance relations is the degree of mutual consultation, confidence, and trust—or the threshold of common danger—which would provide for disparate or competing allied interests to be reconciled, subordinated, or transcended. The machinery is inadequate for hammering out agreement on common global strategies and for working out a better sharing of decision-making as well as burdens in support of those strategies. Halting progress has in fact been made in this direction in recent years, partly as a result of independent but mutually tolerable allied initiatives in African and Middle Eastern affairs, and more uneasily in allied relations with the Soviet Union. More needs to be done to achieve more effective employment of aggregate allied weight in the common interest.

Somewhat more deliberately than either the Nixon or Ford Administration, the Carter Administration called early on for a sharing of burdens and responsibilities among the allies. It demanded, for example, concrete allied suport for sanctions against both the Soviet Union and Iran, and for the build-up of both NATO and Japanese military forces as a counterweight to the Soviet buildup and to growing tensions in Southwest and Southeast Asia. As early as the May 1977 NATO summit, Carter obtained commitments to annual real increases of 3 percent, over a five-year period, in NATO defense budgets, although that target is not being met. Japan, starting from a smaller military base, was increasing defense spending by 6 to 8 percent annually during the late 1970s, but has resisted U.S. pressures for substantially increased defense spending. In December 1979, just prior to the Soviet invasion of Afghanistan, NATO agreed to the deployment of longer-range theater missiles in Western Europe.

The Carter Administration also did its share to disrupt allied comity and confidence. One example was its handling of the neutron or enhanced-radiation warhead for deployment in Western Europe, primarily as a NATO defense against a massed Soviet tank offensive. Encountering initial resistance from several NATO partners against deployment of the weapon on their territory, the Administration pressed hard for a favorable decision. Soon after the West German government agreed to accept the weapon (at some domestic political risk), Carter decided to continue development but delay deployment of the weapon, much to the embarrassment of the West German leadership. On other occasions the Carter Administration took decisions unilaterally, without prior consultation with allies—a criticism that was also leveled against earlier presidents, including Kennedy, Johnson, and Nixon. In fairness, none of the allies has in the past been consistently courageous in embracing political, economic, or military costs of a united allied response to Soviet pressure and threats. Indeed, the European allies have typically been equally critical of the exercise of strong U.S. leadership as they have of the absence of it.

The security treaties which link the industrial democracies of the Atlantic and the Pacific express both the common interest in maintaining a stable world power balance and the substantial combined resources for doing so. NATO plus Japan, Australia, and New Zealand possess between five and six times the productive economic capacity of the communist bloc. Effectiveness of the alliance ultimately derives, however, from orchestration of this combined power in support of common objectives. That, in turn, is largely a function of skillful and consistent American leadership.

Alone among the allies, the United States is conceded and has accepted global responsibilities, including the responsibility of maintaining a strategic deterrent umbrella over the alliance (the pretentions of an "independent" French deterrent notwithstanding). Issues of cooperation within the treaty "boundaries" of, for example, NATO and the U.S.-Japan Security Treaty have traditionally involved close political and defense cooperation and negotiated levels of allied defense spending and support for the maintenance of U.S. troops on allied soil. Allied cooperation outside treaty boundaries has not traditionally been taken for granted, although at times it has been smooth and productive, as in subordinate but strong U.S. support for Britain's successful negotiations legitimating an independent, multiracial government in Zimbabwe in 1980.

Pressures for the alliance to mobilize on broader fronts of common global concern have increased steadily, however, since the 1973 Arab-Israeli war, which led to the Arab oil embargo and the continuing crisis of oil supply and pricing. These pressures grew more urgent with the steady build-up of Soviet offensive military power, from Central Europe to the Far East, and the conquest of Indochina by Soviet-supported Vietnamese troops. The alliance's ability to act cohesively has been stiffened by the Soviet invasion of Afghanistan, followed in short order by convulsions throughout the Arab Middle East and the specter of a Soviet-Warsaw Pact invasion of Poland.

Following Iran's seizure of American hostages and, one month later, the Soviet invasion of Afghanistan, the Carter Administration applied strong pressures on America's major allies, NATO and Japan, to impose sanctions against both Iran and the Soviet Union. After some backing and filling, the allies agreed to cooperate beyond initial expectations, but short of what Carter had requested. (Only Japan and West Germany, among the leading allies, observed the Olympic boycott, for example.) Limited allied sanctions against Iran were adopted, it is widely assumed, primarily as a gesture of support, but also to discourage the president from unilateral military action, such as a naval blockade or mining of Iran's ports. A more remarkable fact is that, however raggedly, NATO did for the first time close ranks in a show of solidarity to punish Soviet (and Iranian)

behavior *outside NATO boundaries.* Equally remarkable is the
fact that Japan for the first time joined Western Europe and the
United States in a concerted diplomatic response to a threat to
the collective security of the democracies.

Allied solidarity was shot through with misgivings, however,
including doubts that "tightening the screws" on Iran would
speed the release of the hostages or pave the way for dealing
constructively with Iran and its Gulf neighbors beyond the
resolution of the hostage issue. Doubts were also expressed that
trade sanctions and the Olympic boycott, while causing some
inconvenience to the Soviet Union, added up to a meaningful
strategy for getting Soviet troops out of Afghanistan or for
deterring future Soviet aggression in the vicinity of the Gulf.

All the allies have rendered political support (and some,
material military support) to the U.S. build-up in the Gulf
region. However, perspectives within the alliance have dif-
fered in the past, and may again, where perceived national
interests (oil-import dependence, profitable trade with the East
bloc, or proximity to intimidating Soviet power) appear to be
jeopardized by the U.S. approach to the problem—or where
the U.S. approach is viewed as misguided or futile.

Forcible eviction of Soviet troops from Afghanistan is not
within the military competence of the United States and its
allies, even were there perfect cohesion within the alliance. The
diplomatic alternative—a negotiated political settlement predi-
cating the Soviet withdrawal on, say, a restoration of Afghanistan's independence and neutrality under international
guarantees—seems equally unpromising, unless the costs to the
Soviet Union of its continuing occupation are made exorbitant.
Those costs could be raised by external military aid to the
Afghan freedom fighters and by organized economic and po-

litical pressures from much of the rest of the world, including the Islamic nations. Islam, however, is itself divided, and some of the issues dividing it—among them, Arab-Israeli conflicts and inter-Arab political and religious rivalries—are being effectively exploited by Soviet military largesse, including the training and equipping of Arab terrorists. Coherent U.S. and allied strategies in the Middle East are confounded by the Gordian complexities of regional politics, exemplified by the more than thirty years of frustrated efforts to achieve a just and stable Arab-Israeli peace.

Perhaps the greatest single diplomatic achievement of the Carter Administration was the midwifing of the Camp David agreements, which led to the signing of the Egyptian-Israeli peace treaty in March 1979. The immediate significance of this treaty was to eliminate for the near future the possibility of a fifth Arab-Israeli war—and the potentially disastrous consequences of such a war for Israel, and for the United States and its allies, in a second and more sweeping Arab oil embargo or a much more direct Soviet intervention than in the past on the Arab side.

However, subsequent Egyptian-Israeli negotiations, under the Carter Administration's persistent prodding, failed to resolve the core of the dispute, which is the political and territorial claims of the Palestinian Arabs. Integral parts of this stalemated question are the form and extent of Palestinian self-determination, the legality of continuing Israeli colonization of occupied Arab territories, the future status of Jerusalem (which Israel proclaimed in 1980 its indivisible and permanent capital), and Israel's return to approximately its pre-1967 borders, in accordance with UN Security Council Resolution 242. Stalemating of the negotiations launched at Camp David has further divided the Arab states, caused stresses in NATO relations, and strained the traditional U.S. friendship with the moderate and conservative Arab regimes.

These Arab-U.S. strains have greatly hampered U.S. diplomatic maneuverability (and military freedom of action) in dealing with the Iranian and Afghanistan crises and in securing allied interests in the Gulf during the Iraq-Iran war, even though the United States continues to exercise greater political leverage in the Arab Middle East—and the Islamic world—than any other major power. Nor are these strains likely to be eased as long as the United States is unable to deliver on Arab presumptions that Washington possesses even greater leverage over Israeli Government policy. The fulcrum which limits that leverage is of course domestic American politics.

American flexibility on the Palestinian question has also been limited by a 1975 Kissinger commitment to Israel not to accept the Palestinian Liberation Organization (PLO) as a bargaining partner, or to communicate diplomatically with the PLO, until the PLO subscribes to Resolution 242 and explicitly recognizes Israel's right to exist. The Israeli Government has also been ambiguous on 242, however, asserting unilateral rights to annex and/or colonize and administer occupied territory. As long as territorial issues remain in dispute and Palestinian political rights are unrealized, U.S. diplomatic and security objectives in the region will continue to be frustrated by the politics of Arab-Arab as well as Arab-Israeli confrontation, fanaticism, and terrorism.

Paradoxically, therefore, what may have been the greatest diplomatic achievement of the Carter Administration, the Egyptian-Israeli peace treaty, has both furthered the ends and complicated the means of U.S. diplomacy in the ongoing Middle

East crises. Symbolic of this dilemma was the Carter Administration's politically costly (at home and abroad) "flip-flop" on the March 1, 1980, UN Security Council resolution condemning the establishment of new Israeli settlements in occupied territories, including East Jerusalem. The United States first backed the resolution, then disavowed its vote, saying it had been cast through a misunderstanding resulting from a failure in communications.

In the interests of regional stability and peace, the energy security of the industrial democracies, the limiting of Soviet penetration of the Middle East, and maintenance of the global power balance, the cutting of this knot has to be high on the agenda of the Reagan Administration. Whether the stalemate is overcome by expanding the Camp David formulas to draw Jordan and conceivably Syria into the negotiations, or by some other formula which leaves the Egyptian-Israeli peace treaty in place, the solution will almost certainly entail firm U.S. insistence on more conciliatory Israeli policies toward Palestinian political and territorial rights, a position all the U.S. allies are certain to support.

Notes

1. In an ABC-TV New Year's interview at the end of his third year in the White House, Carter confessed that the Soviet invasion of Afghanistan "has made a more dramatic change in my opinion of what the Soviet's ultimate goals are than anything they have done in the previous time that I have been in office."

2. A two-year study of U.S. public opinion and U.S. foreign policy, commissioned by the Charles F. Kettering Foundation and released January 5, 1978, indicated 71 percent public support for a SALT agreement as the most important U.S. goal in Soviet relations, overwhelming support for détente and expanded East-West trade,

and only one-third support for U.S. intervention for the purpose of "protecting smaller countries against foreign aggression" or "stopping wars between smaller countries." Promotion of human rights and restraining arms transfers abroad (both Carter objectives) had broad public support. At the same time, about two thirds of the public rated "stopping communism" as a "very important" foreign-policy goal, and felt that the Soviet Union could not be trusted to live up to agreements we make with them. Interestingly, the survey indicated that the better-educated and more affluent sectors of the public were less ideologically opposed to the Soviet Union and more ideologically supportive of human rights.

3. Richard Nixon, *U.S. Foreign Policy for the 1970's, Shaping A Durable Peace—A Report to the Congress, May 3, 1973* (Washington, D.C.: U.S. Government Printing Office), pp. 26–27.

V Rebuilding a Bipartisan Foreign-Policy Consensus

TRADITIONALLY, THE American people offer nonpartisan support to the commander in chief when he declares a situation to be a threat to the nation's security or to its vital international interests, and calls on Congress and the nation to respond accordingly under his leadership.

Such was the nation's mood when President Carter called for measured responses to the invasion of Afghanistan. The more difficult task of presidential leadership is to sustain—through continuing dialogue and negotiation with public opinion—popular support for a strategy that may have to be pursued, not just for months, but for years, at considerable domestic inconvenience and foreign risk, and with no guarantee of early and visible rewards.

An immediate and solvable crisis presents no such problem. A classic case of this kind was the 1962 Soviet attempt to emplace strategic missiles secretly in Cuba. For fourteen days of threatened nuclear holocaust the nation stood fast while President Kennedy mobilized enormous U.S. naval and air power, and great diplomatic skill, to force a Soviet withdrawal. (The modest U.S. concession: assurances it would not intervene militarily in Cuba, as it had attempted unsuccessfully to do the previous year.) Then it was over, and the nation returned to its normal, mostly domestic, preoccupations.

There had been a similar rallying around the presidency (and the United Nations, as agent of global collective security) in Korea in 1950. In the mid-1960s there were dutiful but progressively more qualified rallyings of bipartisan support at successive stages of escalation in the Vietnam conflict.

Unlike the Cuban missile crisis, however, Korea and Vietnam—the two costliest applications of the postwar containment strategy—presented the American people with much more attenuating tests of their endurance, remoter and more ambiguous aims, and no prospect of a clean, precise moment of victory, when the nation could return to its usual affairs. The lessons of this distinction are pertinent as President Reagan and his advisers contemplate what Congress and the American people will now be asked to do in response to the Soviet challenge—at what risks and costs, for what aims, for how long, and whether with the prospect of measurable success down the road.

In both Korea and Vietnam, one issue on which bipartisan support of the war effort broke down was the question of what would constitute success for U.S. arms and strategy. In both conflicts, U.S. aims were limited. They were: to deny the Northern aggressor the conquest of the people and territory of the South; to proceed from a military stalemate to a negotiated and internationally ratified peace settlement on the basis of the *status quo ante*; and, in time and perhaps unrealistically, to promote a peaceful reunification of the divided nations through internationally supervised free elections.

Yet in both Korea and Vietnam, a vocal segment of American public opinion bitterly resented "tying the hands of the military," and limiting U.S. war aims to something less than total destruction of the enemy's war-making capability. Another and ultimately commanding sector of public opinion was increasingly repelled, in both wars, by the human costs of pursuing limited and ambiguous objectives. The containment strategy that was severely tested in Korea was in the end discredited in Vietnam. In the precarious but not yet fully defined situation in which the United States now finds itself vis-à-vis the Soviet Union, a repetition of this erosion of national will is not inconceivable, whether from the fatigue of indecisive combat or from the enervation of preparing for a military struggle that never comes.

The establishment of a significant U.S. military presence in the Middle East, measures now under way to improve U.S. rapid-deployment capabilities, and the commitment to an accelerated build-up of U.S. strategic and conventional power imply a readiness—for the first time since 1974—to commit U.S. military forces to combat under certain circumstances. What all those circumstances might be cannot practically be catalogued in advance. Yet if the national readiness is to be sustained and steadily improved, the American people will need to understand and support the broad political aims and strategic purposes this build-up and deployment are intended to serve.

What coherent and popularly supportable national strategies can be assembled from the wreckage of both containment and détente? Are there new and defensible lines that should be drawn to deter or contain future Soviet expansion, and what sort of issues remain open to negotiation and accommodation? Or, put another way, to what extent will future superpower relations be governed by continuing, open-ended arms competition, and to what extent by mutual efforts to regulate the arms race and stabilize the power balance, while waging the ideological competition by nonmilitary means? Indeed, will American public opinion provide sustained support for anything less than a multilevel strategy?

The cold-war competition has been continuous for longer than a generation; it will in all probability continue for at least another generation. As the gap in U.S.-USSR military power has narrowed, and the technologies of instant and total war have advanced, the Soviet reach has become bolder, and the possibilities of war by overrreach or miscalculation have increased. This calculus suggests that an American foreign policy for the 1980s must incorporate two seemingly contradictory strategies, both of which have substantial but not necessarily overlapping constituencies in public opinion.

The first imperative is to restore a stable global power balance so the Soviet Union will have to weigh more cautiously the risks of future expansionist forays and of further challenges to vital U.S. interests.

The second imperative is to seek to reinforce and institutionalize the stability of the power balance at levels which are not advantageous to the Soviet Union or disadvantageous to the United States and which may gradually moderate the function of raw power confrontation in the competition. This entails resuming negotiations on regulating the arms race, imposing verifiable ceilings on strategic weapons, suppressing or deferring the deployment of destabilizing weapons technologies, and perhaps in time making actual reductions in arms levels.

Yet the balancing and regulating of power are but preventive strategies in a foreign policy that should be designed to achieve positive American goals. Nor do the American people as a whole view it as a binary world, in which all the nation's principal aims can be reduced to the equation of the superpower competition.

It may be that the most dynamic and even promising areas of U.S.-Soviet competition are not the territories, populations, and armaments under direct governance of the two superpowers, but the wider, more diverse, and more complex world, especially the developing "nonaligned" nations of the third world, where two thirds of the human race live. Here is where the competition is being waged most openly, and—given the strategic value to both sides of such areas as the Middle East—it is in the third world that the ultimate U.S.-Soviet military explosion could be ignited. But America's purposes in the third world must be kept larger and more creative than cold-war simplicities.

The most creative and potentially most significant unfinished work awaiting the United States and its allies would need to be done whether or not the formidable Soviet challenge existed; it is simply that much more urgent because of the East-West power struggle. This is the job of patiently shaping a more stable, open, and pluralist world order, based on the fundamental mutual interests of the industrial democracies and the developing nations—interests that are *not* shared between the Soviet Union and the peoples (or even most of the regimes) of the developing third world. These interests include mutual respect for sovereignty and territorial integrity, nonuse of force, cultivation of mutually beneficial economic relations, and construction of an open and integrated world economy in which the benefits of global economic growth are more equitably distributed through fair access to each other's goods, markets, capital, technology, and know-how.

Implicit in this still-distant perception is a recognition that the sharing of interests implies also a sharing of certain values.

At a bare minimum, an integrated and stable world order requires common adherence to international treaty and customary law, and general participation in the development of international institutions to regulate relations, conciliate disputes, and organize sanctions against outlawry.

Rudiments of a world-order system have laboriously been built up over centuries, and the loose institutional framework for integrating the international system has been elaborated profusely during the postwar decades in the literally hundreds of specialized multilateral bodies and agreements that have been invented to manage specific economic, political, and administrative concerns of groups of governments or of the world community. The problem that is least responsive to multilateral persuasion is the problem of defiantly renegade regimes that resort to force, condone or engage in international terrorism, commit genocide, systematically violate human rights, or repudiate international obligations and commitments.

Whatever the ultimate prospects for strengthening the structure of a more stable world order, they undoubtedly rest on the further development of fundamental common interests among states and, for the near term, between the advanced industrial democracies and the developing nations. In the range of U.S. policies addressed to these interests, the two most controversial— long prior to the recent Administration—have been the array of economic policies concerned with third-world development and the gradually evolving policy on human rights.

Economics of World Stability

Accustomed to thinking of their national economy as all but marginally self-sufficient, the American people are still in shock from the forced recognition of their critical dependence on imported oil—moreover, on oil imported from third-world countries, several of which are politically hostile to the United States, and most of which are politically fragile targets of Soviet power diplomacy. The dependence is even broader. The third world provides the United States with critical supplies of such essential defense-related minerals as chrome, tungsten, and titanium.

The growing U.S. dependence works also in the other direction. The developing countries have in recent years become the fastest-growing markets in the world for American exports, investments, and profits. This fact belies the familiar complaint that three decades of U.S. aid, technical assistance, private investment, and trade expansion in the third world have been unproductive. On the contrary, the overall effort, however erratically executed over the years, has been resoundingly successful. At least a half-dozen developing economies that have benefited from American aid and investment have reached the takeoff point of self-sustained economic growth, on the basis of free enterprise, and during the 1970s registered the highest sustained rates of annual GNP growth in the world. At least a dozen other developing countries are in the wings, preparing to join the act.

Building on these successes, to strengthen the momentum of world economic development and integration, is a most practical and promising U.S. (and allied) strategy for the 1980s. It will have its costs in the adjustment of business, labor, and congressional attitudes toward third-world trade, investment, and aid. (The United States ranks about thirteenth in the world in the value of foreign aid as a percentage of GNP.) Patience will also be required, for the progress is slow and uncertain, and there are inevitable conflicts and contradictions, in such a strategy, between U.S. economic (both public and private) and political objectives. Yet the potential rewards, both economic and political, justify the effort.

A third world in which there were a preponderance of self confidently independent, increasingly prosperous, and internally progressive and stable trading partners, linked in their basic interests to the democracies, would constitute a positive and powerful weight in the global power balance and a stronger foundation for a stable world order. It should also be a more favorable environment for the flourishing of freedom and human rights.

Human Rights

Since the 1950s, successive Administrations of both parties have been criticized for (1) cynically embracing ruthless dictators (from Nicaragua's Anastasio Somoza to the Shah of Iran), usually on grounds of their reliability as anticommunists and as friendly hosts to U.S. private investment; (2) cynically abandoning staunch U.S. friends (again from Somoza to the Shah) when their tenure was under internal siege; or (3) embracing left-leaning revolutionary regimes that may also be receiving aid and comfort from adversaries of the United States.

The policy dilemmas are real. Considerations of *Realpolitik* and hard national interest may at times be overriding, as they were indisputably when the alliance with the Soviet Union hastened the defeat of Hitler. There are also times and places where applying absolutist human-rights standards is not only bullheaded and futile in terms of liberalizing results, but also dangerous to longer-term U.S. and alliance interests. In South Korea and Brazil, for example, the pace of democratization may be accelerated over time by U.S. pressures, but it cannot be commanded. In NATO ally Turkey, the military government that seized power in 1980 may well turn out to be a more effective caretaker of democracy than the elected but terrorist-paralyzed government it replaced—provided the caretaking is temporary, internal order is restored without violating human rights, and political leadership learns from the transition experience. There are risks.

Yet it is a curious myth that the United States has no right or obligation to attempt to influence sane economic and humane social and political policies in a country with which it shares close economic and security interests, and ongoing programs of intergovernmental cooperation. Limiting U.S. concerns to, for example, the training of security forces and insuring the friendly treatment of U.S. business investments in a state whose government consistently violates the human rights of its citizens is a perniciously selective form of intervention. A regime of the right or left that oppresses its own people is inherently unstable and an undependable ally or investment market.

An American foreign policy that is neutral on the issues of human rights—in the Soviet bloc, in allied and friendly nations, and around the world—would be out of joint with America's historic values and would be perceived at home and abroad as hypocritically flawed. Alliances with regimes serve important, sometimes transient state interests; alliances with peoples and their aspirations build, in the long run, the most enduring foundations for cooperation and alliance.

The United States has been, for more than two centuries, the most revolutionary model influencing world history. Its record in promoting human rights, at home as well as abroad, is mixed, but on balance it is a good and decent record. In just the last four years, admitting the excesses and deficiencies in the conduct of congressionally mandated human-rights policies, the conditions and status of human rights in the world have improved. During those years there has been a resurgence of democracy in northern South America (apart from Guyana); Brazil and possibly Uruguay are veering closer to democratic norms; and the prospects for broadly based democratic governance have improved in Jamaica and may have a slimly better chance in Central America.

In this same period, the number of multiparty democracies in Africa has risen from two to at least seven, including the most populous nation on the continent, Nigeria, which has opted for an approximately Madisonian solution to the problems of an ethnically diverse and "geographically extended republic." India, despite the return to power of the sometime authoritarian Mrs. Indira Gandhi, has reestablished claim to its title of the world's most populous democracy.

Even China, with one quarter of the world's population, and in a shambles left by political and economic mismanagement under Mao, has been stumbling toward the pragmatism of greater freedom of initiative and institutionalization of legal rights, out of the practical needs of its modernization program.

Finally, the spontaneous uprising of Polish workers in the late summer of 1980 floodlighted more brightly than Afghanistan— or even than Hungary in 1956 and Czecholslovakia in 1968— the linkage between repression of freedom and human rights on the one hand and, on the other, the self-enervating inhumanity, inefficiency, and failure of the Soviet model for national development and international order. In the first instance, the Polish uprising was a proletarian rebellion (in a proletarian paradise) against the gross incompetence and corruption of the

Polish communist party's mismanagement of the economy—complaints which had to be and were acknowledged, and which resulted in extraordinary purges of party hacks from the Politburo down to district and factory levels. In the second instance, whether or not initially intended, it was interpreted in both the communist and noncommunist worlds as a mass repudiation of the structure and consequences of a political system that is regimented by a self-perpetuating elite which reserves to itself a monopoly of power and privilege.

The audacity of that challenge to Marxist-Leninist doctrine, and inferentially to Soviet hegemony in Eastern Europe, may have doomed the Polish Solidarity movement from the moment its power to force changes in Polish communist party governance became evident. Whether the promised party reforms (including rotation of leadership and secret balloting for top party posts) are allowed to go into effect, and Solidarity survives under constraints to its political power, or whether the entire movement is suppressed, it is predictable that the Soviet Union will not permit an independent political force to function within its domain. The infection to be quarantined is freedom, lest the rest of Eastern Europe and the Soviet Union itself be "Polonized."

Because freedom is the uncompromisable divider between superpower concerns, interests, and purposes—as well as for all the positive reasons that relate to world order, stability, and justice—the commitment to freedom and the promotion of human rights must continue to occupy a prominent place in American foreign policy.

These are among the lessons of the past that need to be incorporated into the blueprinting of an American foreign policy for the 1980s—strategies capable of enlisting broad and durable bipartisan support at home, and respect abroad. There are other lessons, including the obvious needs to restore domestic economic growth at stable prices and to reduce as rapidly as possible U.S. (and allied) dependence on imported energy, if the United States is to meet its national-security and alliance responsibilities, while also meeting the expectations of the American people for full employment and a better future for all of America's children.

America's strengths, whether for domestic or foreign purposes, are indivisible. Only by mobilizing all of the nation's strengths, moral as well as material, and political as well as military, will the American people be in a position to meet the immediate and future challenges with restored national self-confidence.

A popularly supportable foreign policy will consist of a brace of strategies which are consistent with America's most deeply cherished values, balance domestic and international priorities, are perceived to be within America's reach, offer reasonable prospect that they can be implemented, are more likely to lead to peace than to war—but accept the risk of war as a price for keeping the peace—and focus as much on what America is for as on what it is against.

In summarizing the principal elements of such a program, what America is *for* is the appropriate place to begin.

VI Applying the Lessons to the 1980s

Recapturing the Initiative for Freedom

THE CRITICAL contest between the United States and the Soviet Union is not how the Soviet Union is to be governed, but how the future world order is to be organized. In that contest, the Soviet Union claims the right and responsibility—as agent of the inexorable laws of history—to use all available means, including force, not only to extend its system of governance to other states, but also—as in Hungary, Czechoslovakia, Afghanistan, and Poland—to prevent the defection of any society once it has crossed the ideological divide. History, according to the Brezhnev Doctrine, is irreversible, and its momentum is with the Soviet Union.

Freedom is the issue.

Yet, unlike its ideological adversary, freedom is not a dogma which explains or justifies any concentration of power or any orthodoxy of belief. It is a unifying principle only because it provides cohesion and security for diversity. Because the idea of freedom is inherently plural, it is more readily demonstrated than defined.

Freedom—both freedom from and freedom to—is the most basic of America's values, the standard by which virtually all the rights and responsibilities of the citizen are tested. Freedom is practiced in the observance of human rights, civil liberties, freedom of speech and worship, equality before the law, due process, rights of conscience and privacy, government by consent of the governed, and tolerance for peaceful dissent.

These are among the traditional values that have made the American polity a permanent revolutionary force in history. It has been a conservative revolution in that it has sought to sustain and perfect received values and established institutions, at home and abroad. It has been for the most part a nonideological revolution in that it has protected pluralism and promoted mutual tolerance more consistently than it has attempted to enforce conformity. It has also been a liberalizing revolution because of innate sensitivity to injustice, and recognition of the need for continuing reform, at home and abroad.

Potentially the most powerful nonmilitary weapon in the global ideological struggle is the irrepressible yearning, even inside the Soviet empire, for greater freedom. Deploying this weapon effectively is an option available to the liberalizing American revolutionary model, not to the repressive Soviet model. Recapturing the initiative for freedom in this struggle means vigorously asserting America's revolutionary role in the world in support for the independence and self-determination of all nations; respect for international law, treaties, and agreements; and the strengthening of human rights and democratic institutions and processes throughout the world.

Refusing to engage in, or disengaging from, this ideological battle, for whatever reasons of diplomatic linkage, is tantamount to deserting the battlefield that is second in importance only to an actual test of arms. The prize for effectively engaging in ideological warfare is the exposure and discrediting of Soviet pretensions that the repression of freedom, rather than its enlargement, is the wave of the future.

One of the most useful but controversial intergovernmental forums for recapturing the initiative for freedom is the continuing international review of compliance with the Helsinki Accords. The accords were signed in 1975 by the heads of thirty-five governments—all European governments except Albania, but including the Soviet Union and all its Warsaw Pact allies, and the United States and Canada. The accords are not a treaty, and provide for no enforcement measures. However, the review process mandated by the accords holds each signatory publicly accountable for faithful compliance with each and every provision.

Initially proposed by the Soviet Union, the Helsinki agreements call for ("basket one") cooperation on maintaining European peace and security, including a pledge not to alter existing European borders by force and a general repudiation of the use of force anywhere; expansion of East-West economic cooperation ("basket two") and, at the insistence of NATO and neutral powers, freedom of contact and movement of peoples and mutual observance of various human rights, including reuniting of families, freedom to emigrate, noninterference with journalists, and the freer flow of information ("basket three").

At both review conferences to date, in Belgrade in 1978 and Madrid in 1980-81, the Soviet and East European governments resorted to every available parliamentary device and intimidation to obstruct foreign discussion of systematic violations by the communist bloc of basket-three agreements, including persecution of their own citizens who had set up committees to monitor human-rights compliance by their governments. Soviet-bloc spokesmen also expressed outrage that the repre-

sentatives of nearly every other signatory government con-
demned the Soviet invasion of Afghanistan as a violation of the
nonuse-of-force pledge in the accords. The criticisms were
dismissed as interference in the internal affairs of Afghanistan
and contravention of the spirit of détente embodied in the
accords.

Max M. Kampelman, co-chairman of the U.S. delegation to
CSCE, responded that, "If détente as a concept is to be interpreted one way by us and another way by the Soviet Union,
then it is a meaningless word which cannot govern our relationships." He added:

Our ideological differences are sharp. It would be folly for us to
consider it realistic that we can persuade one another of the virtues of
our respective beliefs. We, in America, do not shrink from the
competition of ideas. Americans are as free to read the works of Marx
and Lenin as to read the works of Franklin and Jefferson; all are
available in our bookstores and libraries. . . . We are as free to listen
to Radio Moscow as to our own networks. Does a Soviet citizen have
the same freedom? To ask the question is to answer it.

We believe that, in the long run, the aspirations of mankind toward
greater individual freedom will inevitably be attained, and cannot be
defeated no matter how severe the repression. Helsinki monitors may
be arrested in Moscow, but in doing so they create a situation in which
those of us all over the world who cherish human freedom join our
voices with theirs and become with them Helsinki monitors.

We are convinced that the historic inevitability for the human
being is the inevitability of human rights, of individual freedom, and
not of some ideologically defined doctrinal concept of revolution.[1]

A number of American political leaders have urged U.S.
renunciation of the Helsinki Accords and withdrawal from
CSCE as "punishment" of the Soviet Union for its behavior in
Afghanistan, in Poland, or in general. The more effective

punishment would be to keep alive for as long as the Soviet Union can tolerate it a useful forum where specific and detailed examples of Soviet conduct that is cynically in violation of its formal international and its own constitutional commitments can be held up to the harsh scrutiny of world opinion. Let the Soviet Union bear the onus of fleeing that scrutiny.

The defense and promotion of freedom in the world is too large and sensitive a task for government alone. America makes its purposes known to the world, not solely through official acts and statements, but also through the spontaneous voices of its labor leaders, businessmen, exchange students and professors, military personnel, and tourists, and through its mass communications and entertainment media. The unfettered diversity of these many private views and voices is another demonstration of what Americans cherish as freedom.

The free flow of ideas and information across national borders is becoming, with each new advance in communications technology, increasingly difficult to inhibit or control. This insures that the world marketplace of ideas will continue to be competitive. Yet the totalitarian mind continues to seek means of controlling the international flow, through both governmental and intergovernmental codes and restraints. These campaigns must be resisted, not just by the U.S. Government, but also by the independent nongovernmental news services in the world, whose contributions to international awareness, understanding, and cooperation are best secured when their professional competence is free of regulation, censorship, or intimidation.

There are other ways in which the private sector in its diversity augments and complements governmental programs for the promotion of freedom. For example, for more than a generation the Freedom Radios (Radio Free Europe and Radio Liberty, broadcasting in local languages to the peoples of Eastern Europe and the Soviet Union) have complemented the official broadcasts of the Voice of America. Alexander Solzhenitsyn has called the combination of these official and unofficial radios potentially "the mightiest weapon that the United States possesses to create a mutual understanding (or even an alliance) between America and the oppressed Russian people."[2]

The survival and flourishing of freedom in the world is not ordained by any law of history or nature. It depends on the vitality and determination of a diversity of free peoples, and on the yearning of the not free to be free. The Reagan Administration should not let slip the opportunity to forge these forces into an alliance, and to lead it.

Investing in World Order

The advanced industrial democracies share a fundamental self interest in the strengthening of international law and institutions, and in promoting within this framework the economic and social modernization, social stability, and political respectability of the emerging nations of the world. Indeed, the democracies have consistently provided the institutional models, the bulk of the capital and technology, the managerial know-how, the export markets, and the security umbrella that have enabled those "new" nations with the basic resources, and competent domestic leadership, to develop their economies and, in a growing number of cases, to prosper.

Relations between the first and third worlds have been complicated by postcolonial resentments and by misjudgments and insensitivities on both sides. Inequities in the terms of trade, especially between raw materials and manufactured goods, have long been a source of contention, contributing in the case of oil to creation of the most powerful cartel in history. Interjection of cold-war military and ideological competition into third-world politics has created particularly dangerous complexities for the democracies—especially Soviet, Cuban, North Korean, and East European military support for third-world guerrillas and terrorists.

The United States, because of its uniquely global responsibilities and its traditional ethical concerns, must cope with a special set of contradictions in its relations with the third world. In several cases, it shares important strategic, economic, and other interests with countries—the Republic of Korea, the Philippines, South Africa, Argentina, and Chile, for example—where democratic principles and human rights are in varying degrees violated or suppressed. U.S. policy-makers find there is no simple rheostat for adjusting the appropriate degrees of political intimacy or coolness which might encourage liberalization by such governments, without at the same time risking important state interests.

It is a dilemma that can neither be avoided nor managed in simple, absolute terms. The United States lacks the power to dictate the domestic political practices of foreign regimes, but it has the obligation under international convention as well as domestic tradition to register its disapproval of official repression and violence, and to do so evenhandedly whether the regime is rightist or leftist or in other respects friendly or hostile. In the case of ostensibly friendly regimes, the U.S. Government should use whatever liberalizing influence it may have, whether quietly or publicly, and in any event should not provide police training or equipment to carry out repressive policies, or offer other gratuitous evidence it condones those policies.

Under some circumstances, the United States can merge its concerns for democracy and human rights with the organized expressions of such concern by international forums, such as the Inter-American Human Rights Commission of the Organization of American States (OAS) or the Helsinki review process of the CSCE. UN bodies, unfortunately, do not often provide a useful platform for these issues, because of the arithmetic of irresponsible political views built into the UN General Assembly and the Specialized Agencies. Whatever the means, the purposes of the strategy should be clear and consistent: to promote freedom and human rights and to strengthen democratic institutions and international law throughout the world.

One self-serving purpose of expanded and more coherent U.S. and allied support for democratic development in the third world is, of course, to reduce the vulnerability of these societies to internal or external destabilization, and especially to Soviet manipulation. The more fundamental and longer-range purpose is to assist these countries to enter into an expanding and pluralist community of nations, economically viable and self-interestedly interdependent with the democracies, that will respect—and, if possible, share—each other's political values.

Assimilation of even the most advanced and prosperous developing countries into the mainstream political economy of the first world will not be cost-free—in cultural tolerance and patience, in capital outlays and technological sharing, or in domestic economic adjustments to accept the lower-cost manufactured exports of those countries. Both economic and political accommodations will be necessary in order to build bridges to a more open, stable, and cooperative world order of the future.

Strengthening the Alliance

Problems of leadership and followership, and of coherence and continuity of policies, have been as troublesome within the alliance as on the domestic American political scene, and partly for the same reasons. The alliance is also a democratic structure, sharing certain basic values and common purposes. Yet, as in the domestic society, the alliance reflects competing priorities and contradictory assessments of how to meet the Soviet challenge—whether by trying to refurbish détente, by rearming for confrontation, or by some mix of these and other strategies.

In contrast to the American federal system, the alliance is a collection of effectively independent sovereignties, lacking any centralizing political authority, and quite capable of conducting divergent and even competitive foreign policies. In fact, there is not one alliance, but several, of which NATO has habitually been considered the power core. Even within NATO, the third-ranking military power, France, is technically outside the unified military command. Moreover, the Pacific wing of the Atlantic-Pacific alliance is a far looser collection of bilateral mutual-security arrangements between the United States and partners of such disparate capacities and divergent national interests as Japan, Republic of Korea, Australia-New Zealand (linked by the ANZUS Treaty), and the Philippines and Thailand.

Japan, linchpin of the Pacific alliance, has steadily been undertaking larger political and defense responsibilities on behalf of the alliance, although in comparison with other key allies it falls considerably short in defense budgeting of its capacity as the world's second-ranking economic power. Constitutional inhibitions and politics in this most consensual of democratic societies have figured in the studied pace of Japanese rearmament; so have external considerations that are equally pertinent to the Reagan Administration's review of America's Asian strategies.

China has endorsed Japanese rearmament in the context of the U .S.-Japan Security Treaty, both as a bulwarking of the suspect U.S. deterrent against Soviet hegemonic designs in East Asia and as insurance against an independently rearmed Japan, free of U.S. constraints. In a variation on the same theme, South Korea and the Association of Southeast Asian Nations (ASEAN: Indonesia, Malaysia, the Philippines, Singapore, and Thailand)—while welcoming Japanese (and U.S.) aid, investment and trade as essential to their continuing economic progress—are almost as fearful of a militarily powerful and Asian-dominant Japan as they are of Soviet, Soviet-backed Vietnamese, or Chinese hegemony in their region.

Much less clear than the sharp East-West confrontation in Europe, the power balance yet to be constructed in Pacific Asia will be a multisided and nuanced balancing of contradictory interests. It would be hazardous to American interests and alliance purposes to treat the Pacific wing of the alliance in simple Atlantic terms of counterpoise to Soviet power. Neither a China card nor a Japan card will effectively substitute for a progressively more cohesive voluntary alliance of democracies, led by the United States as *primus inter pares*, and unthreatening to regional stability.

Considering the centrifugal forces, it is noteworthy that North America, Western Europe, and Japan have showed the community of purpose and policy they have in response to the succession of common shocks they have had to absorb during the 1970s—especially the 1973–74 Arab oil embargo and subsequent cartel-dictated spiraling of world oil prices, the 1974–75 worldwide recession, the 1974 U.S. withdrawal from Vietnam and the ensuing Vietnamese conquest of the rest of Indochina, the rapid Soviet military build-up in the latter 1970s from Central Europe to the Far East, and the crises in Iran, Afghanistan, and Poland in 1979–80.

As they crossed each new threshold of common danger, the allies accepted greater shares of the alliance burden. At France's initiative, the annual seven-nation economic summits were launched in 1975 (Britain, Canada, France, Italy, Japan, West Germany, and the United States), in an effort to achieve better harmonization of national policies to deal with trade and payments imbalances, energy cooperation, and common problems of inflation, unemployment, and lagging economic growth. Joint progress was also made during the latter 1970s in coordinating third-world development aid, assistance to the refugee explosion in Southeast Asia in particular, and world-trade liberalization under the Tokyo Round of the multilateral trade negotiations of the General Agreement on Tariffs and Trade (GATT). Beginning in 1977, serious attention was addressed to the need for defense modernization and build-up in Western Europe and the Far East, a concern that was nudged by the December 1979 Soviet invasion of Afghanistan and brought to a head a year later by the intimidating Soviet threat to invade Poland.

Debate continues between the United States and its allies on the adequacy of allied contributions to the common defense. In the period 1969–79 Europe's share of NATO defense spending rose from 22.81 percent to 41.65 percent, while the U.S. share fell from 75.4 percent to 56.5 percent. Pentagon officals point out, however, that in terms of percent of GNP none of the European allies (except Britain) or Japan approaches the U.S. 5 percent level. In light of the delicate and possibly deteriorating balance of forces in Central Europe, American defense planners would like the European allies in the next few years to spend less for long-term weapons procurement and more on improving the readiness of existing forces.

Nonetheless, the contributions of individual allies to peacekeeping and peace-building are not inconsiderable. Key allies have undertaken special obligations—political and even military, as well as economic—in areas where they have historic ties and interests. France in Francophone Africa and Britain in Commonwealth countries around the globe are noteworthy examples. Another is Japan, now the primary source of external assistance to the economic modernization programs of China, South Korea and the ASEAN countries. The same three allies have also offered independent political initiatives, beyond U.S. capabilities, on stalemated Middle East issues.

In self-perceptions, if not quite in fact, it is becoming more an alliance of equals, willing to share more equitably the responsibilities for collective security. This maturing is the result both of the improving internal capacity of the allies to contribute to the common effort and of the growing visibility and ominousness of the common external threat. Mobilizing this more mature alliance in support of unified strategic purposes is a formidable challenge to the Reagan Administration. A confrontational approach to the allies, as well as to the common adversary, would be one confrontation too many.

The ultimate U.S. responsibility for maintaining the global power balance and deterrent cannot be delegated. Yet the persuasive validity of U.S. political goals in the world, and the efficacy of the ethical and political values underlying U.S. foreign policy, derive in large measure from the sharing of these goals and values—and the will to defend them—with the community of Atlantic and Pacific democracies.

Possibly the most significant revelation to overtake the allies during 1980 was the inescapable linkage between the year-apart Soviet intrusion into Afghanistan and the Soviet mobilization on Polish borders. With notable exceptions, the allied response to the first event was raggedy, although it was a milestone in that both NATO and Japan acknowledged the need to close ranks (at least *pro forma*) before a common threat occurring outside the geographical area covered by their respective treaty obligations to the United States. The following-on Polish crisis more nearly solidified NATO at its December 1980 Brussels meeting in a fifteen-nation declaration that détente "has been seriously damaged by Soviet actions" and that "it could not survive if the Soviet Union were again to violate the basic rights of any state to territorial integrity and independence." Japan quickly joined in the warning.

The sweep of the Soviet power challenge—from Central Europe through the Middle East, Southwest Asia, and Southeast Asia, to the military build-up in Japan's Soviet-occupied Northern Territories—suggests the irrelevance of the original treaty boundaries. The energy security of Western Europe and Japan will continue throughout the 1980s to depend on maintaining the flow of oil from the Gulf and keeping the sea lanes open from the Gulf westward, around the Cape of Good Hope and through the Atlantic, and eastward, through the Indian Ocean, the Straits of Malacca, the South China Sea, and the Western Pacific. Defense of this allied lifeline is not provided for under existing mutual-security arrangements.

Neither a merging of the principal Atlantic and Pacific alliances, nor the creation of a single super-alliance directorate for the coordination of a unified defense strategy seems practical, unless there is a further and drastic deterioration in the international situation. The time may be propitious, however, for the invention of open-ended machinery for closer continuing consultation and contingency planning among those key allies with the capacity and will to expand and project their contributions to the common defense well beyond their currently defined theaters of responsibility.

Negotiating from Strengths

Failure of the 1970s' détente, as a relationship in which tensions were supposed to have been relaxed and cooperation expanded, does not mean that East-West diplomacy should be suspended or arms-control negotiations abandoned. On the contrary, in this 1980s period of heightened tensions and rising danger, continuing and patient diplomatic communications are needed to prevent misunderstanding or miscalculation and to insure that Soviet leadership recognizes the conditions under which crisis situations can be jointly managed, without armed conflict.

In the same vein, arms-control negotiations need to be sustained, especially during the period of the U.S. and allied defense build-up, in order to avert the reckless endangerment to the world of an uncontrolled arms race.

The diplomacy of crisis management and arms-race management, although certain to be arduous and frustrating, should be continuous because of the one fundamental interest both sides share: avoidance of thermonuclear holocaust. These are not "linkage" issues, to be taken up or put aside on the basis of progress (or lack of it) in other areas of negotiation that may be under way. From the current perspective of the United States and its allies, the one non-negotiable issue is the reestablishment beyond doubt of a stable power balance. How the balance is stabilized, and under what terms the power aspects of the competition will then be pursued, are functions of diplomatic negotiations.

Three practical tests for future SALT negotiations were provided in a Presidential Directive (PD 50) of August 14, 1979: Does the proposal contribute to achieving U.S. defense and force-posture goals? Will it restrain U.S. adversaries and help U.S. allies? Will it truly limit the arms race and actually reduce the likelihood of war? The SALT II treaty negotiated by the Carter Administration is dead, primarily because of the judgment of a number of defense experts, in and outside the Senate, that it did not meet such criteria. In particular, critics felt the treaty would not reduce short-term U.S. vulnerabilities during the first half of the 1980s, nor would it significantly arrest the momentum of the arms race.

Although the Carter Administration had initially tried and failed to win Soviet agreement to substantial cuts in strategic arsenals, that failure need not inhibit the Reagan Administration from reopening the question of a SALT treaty which begins real cutbacks. A SALT agreement, for example, which lowers the ceilings on strategic-missile deployment and reduces the warhead count on both sides, would come closer to meeting the criteria of PD 50. It would do so by improving the survivability and credibility of the U.S. deterrent, while closing the window of U.S. vulnerability in the mid-1980s and reducing the likelihood of war. It could also buy valuable time for the United States and its allies to tool up broader peace-building strategies, capitalizing on vastly superior economic and technological strengths and on the powerful appeal of Western advocacy of an open and pluralist world order based on cooperation rather than force.

Willingness to negotiate with the Soviet Union on other, specific ways to moderate tensions and reduce the dangers of conflict is neither a favor to the Soviet Union nor a sign of weakness—provided the negotiations are conducted in the context of a determined and sustained repairing of current U.S. and allied military deficiencies and progress toward greater alliance cohesion. Weakness lies in the absence of a negotiating strategy which commits real U.S. and allied strengths to clear and reasonable purposes. This most ambitious task, in former Secretary of State Dean Rusk's phrase, of "organizing the peace," calls for progressively closer coordination of allied power and policy.

At the outset, the allies need to reach clearer mutual agreement on the conditions they consider essential for organizing the peace. For starters, the Reagan Administration might seek allied agreement on such elementary terms as the following:

1. that the allies will not permit the Soviet Union to achieve military superiority, nor that margin of intimidating power which would allow it to advance its political aims by blackmail;
2. that the allies, after too long neglect, are resuming their half of the arms race, but that they will welcome at any time meaningful negotiations to arrest and even reverse the arms race, and to stabilize the power balance, through agreements on strategic arms limitations (SALT), mutual and balanced force reductions in Europe (MBFR), a total

ban on nuclear-weapons testing, and other stabilizing measures;

3. that the allies would also consider resuming the normalizing of commercial relations that had been nourished during the 1970s détente, but only on the condition that the Soviet Union observe with comparable assiduousness the other essential components of détente it has formally undertaken in, for example, the Helsinki Accords—including its commitments on the nonuse of force, observance of human rights, unimpeded movement of peoples and information across international borders, ending the jamming of Western radio broadcasts, permitting freer emigration, etc.;

4. that the Brezhnev Doctrine of right of intervention in a "fraternal socialist state" in order to preserve a pro-Soviet regime is unacceptable whether invoked in Eastern Europe, Afghanistan, or elsewhere, and that the principles of nonuse of force, respect for sovereignty and territorial integrity, and right of self-determination of all peoples are universal principles, applicable to relations between all states, and fundamental to an organized and stable peace;

5. and, finally, that the allies will defend their vital common interests, by force if necessary, against future Soviet and Soviet-proxy challenges to those interests.

Spelling out U.S. and allied "peace aims" in terms such as these—and reinforcing their serious intent with appropriate defense and political measures—can hardly be expected to suddenly transform Soviet international behavior, much less convert that repressive and seemingly paranoid system into an open and cooperating member of a pluralist world order. Yet the invitation to move toward these desirable ends should be explicit in the incentives and disincentives built into U.S. and allied negotiating strategies.

Whether external pressures can have any constructive impact on the internal liberalization of the Soviet Union and its dependent East European societies is highly problematical. Overt intervention by Western governments in major East European uprisings has been out of the question since the tragic demonstration in Hungary in 1956 that, even in an era of overwhelming strategic superiority, the United States could not match its "liberation" propaganda with effective material support for the Hungarian freedom fighters. The hands-off policies toward Czechoslovakia in 1968 and Poland in 1980–81 followed accordingly.

Yet irrepressible pressures for liberalization surface periodically within the Soviet imperium, and it is unthinkable that Western governments and private organizations should fail to express common cause with Soviet and East European dissidents whose principal demand is that their governments honor their own constitutional guarantees and international commitments. The gap between myth and reality in Leninist legalism should not be allowed to become blurred, whether inside the Soviet Union, in other communist-run states, or in brutalized Afghanistan.[3]

The alliance is not lacking in economic leverage. The Soviet and (to a lesser extent) Warsaw Pact economies, despite their impressive belt-tightened performance in military-industrial and space-science sectors, are not self-sufficient or internationally competitive in either high technology or such basic sectors as consumer industry and agriculture. They need dependable North American supplies of food and feed grains to improve consumer diets and build their livestock industry. They need

North American, West European, and Japanese technology to modernize their nondefense industries, raise domestic living standards, and efficiently develop and market their less-accessible natural resources, including oil and natural gas. They need Western credits, markets, and long-term commercial contracts to maintain adequate levels of domestic capital formation and international liquidity.[4]

It is a question of no small importance whether these trade-offs—the practical economic requirements of running the communist economies and the claims of communism's subjects for higher economic returns and greater personal liberty—are in some way negotiable between East and West, and, if so, whether publicly or only tacitly. Whether, for example, the domestic Polish political and managerial reforms are permitted to survive at all, and with how much latitude for experiment and the easing of authoritarian restraints, may have something to do with how seriously the Kremlin assesses the desolate state of the Polish economy, including Poland's monumental debt to Western creditors, and the costly burdens the Soviet Union would inherit if the reforms were squashed and the Polish economy were plunged into still deeper trouble.[5]

The overriding consideration, however, is more likely to be the Soviet Union's inablity to compromise on internal political pluralism. Moreover, the Soviet Union has good reason to calculate that an allied strategy of withholding goods and credits would be resisted by Western industrialists, including farmers and bankers, who have been historically reluctant to forego profitable business opportunities. That calculation is enshrined in Lenin's 1921 prediction that the capitalists of the world would "open credit . . . and provide us with the essential materials and technology, thus restoring our military, especially for our future victorious attacks on our suppliers."

It will be a test of the Reagan Administration's leadership of the nation and the alliance whether tough defense and political strategies are undermined by "business as usual" in the economic sphere.

Redefining U.S. Strategic Objectives

Cautions need to be drawn from the nation's trials and confusions, throughout the postwar era, in trying to manage alternating periods of confrontation and détente with the Soviet bloc. Two lessons should by now be beyond debate. These are, first, that the United States has no real choice between isolating itself from and engaging itself fully in this power struggle and, second, that this struggle cannot be evaded or superseded by some diplomatic sleight of hand which discounts the requirement for maintaining the military power balance. Negotiations and accommodations, whether under détente or any other rubric, can be nothing more than the exercise of diplomatic incentives and disincentives to civilize the joint management of the continuing competition.

Another caution to be drawn from the nation's painful experiences in Korea and Vietnam is that U.S. military forces should never again be committed to combat—in threat or in fact—anywhere in the world unless the purposes for which they are committed (1) are vital to U.S. security or explicit in U.S. treaty commitments, (2) are so understood and accepted by the American people (and by America's allies and friends), and (3) are within reach of the forces committed to those purposes.

A further lesson is that open-ended strategic doctrines which imply an automatic U.S. military response to every Soviet expansionist foray (e.g., containment or the Truman Doctrine) had practical utility, if ever, only in an era when overwhelming

U.S. political, economic, and nuclear dominance allowed the United States at least the theoretical capacity to choose the level of its response to any untoward Soviet thrust. That margin of U.S. preeminence can probably never be regained, nor need its irretrievability be lamented.

It has never been, in war or in peace, nor should it ever be, the ambition of the United States to acquire the concentration of power necessary to dominate the entire globe and to command its destiny. It is a proper concern and responsibility of the United States, however, not to concede by default that option to the Soviet Union. It is imperative that the Soviet Union be denied a preponderance of military power, that the global power balance be restored and maintained, and that Soviet leadership be persuaded by power realities, as well as through diplomacy, to reconsider the risks of an expansionist strategy based on force.

American strategies for the 1980s that are at once responsive to the challenge, credible to adversaries as well as allies and friends, and broadly supportable by the American people, will be within these bounds.

Restoring a Stable Power Balance

All of America's important objectives in the world, and indeed the security and perhaps survival of the Republic, require prompt restoration of a credible, stable power balance. The measure of attaining this is not simply the size of the defense budget or the percentage by which it is increased annually in comparison with Soviet defense outlays. Nor is the measure a superpower symmetry of weapon for weapon and man for man. Rather, the measure of both credibility and stability is whether the expansionist pattern of Soviet behavior begins to be moderated in recognition of the U.S. capacity and will to resist, repel, or punish that behavior.

The continuing mission of U.S. military forces is defensive rather than aggressive, deterrent and retaliatory rather than preemptive. This means that a stable power balance does not lie in arithmetical trade-offs of men and weapons which produce a paper parity in defenses, but leave the Soviet Union with certain offensive advantages which are immune to U.S. countermeasures. Parity based on that equation is inherently unstable.

Because of the differences in missions, the United States should seek (as Presidential Directive 50 implies) a more realistic parity based on probable political consequences of the balance-of-defense postures. This suggests a sufficient *qualitative edge in U.S. strategic power* to neutralize Soviet attempts to employ nuclear blackmail against other states, and a sufficient *edge of flexibility and mobility in U.S. and allied conventional forces* to deter excessive Soviet risk-taking in conflict with vital U.S. and allied interests around the world.

There are other implications of this defense strategy, including a high degree of invulnerablity in retaliatory (i.e., deterrent) power, effective anti-antisatellite capabilities to protect reconnaissance and communications systems, improved defenses (civilian as well as military) against chemical and biological warfare, and other measures appropriate to an essentially defensive rather than offensive military posture. It may also be advisable to plan and prepare to implement, as a contribution to the credibility of the U.S. deterrent, a civil and industrial defense program appropriate to the 1980s.

Former Secretary of Defense (1969–73) Melvin R. Laird summarized "The question now before the new administration." It is:

. . . by how much and how quickly the budget should be increased and to what areas the increment should be applied. What is needed now is a defense budget that not only will help us deal with our deficiencies in a prudent manner, but is also so economically feasible and politically supportable that it can be sustained over the long haul. Two decades of neglect cannot be undone in five years.

The worst thing that can happen is for the nation to go on a defense spending binge that will create economic havoc at home and confusion abroad and that cannot be dealt with wisely by the Pentagon. For example, a 12-percent-a-year increase in the defense budget over the next five years will result in a $400 billion defense budget by FY86. Such an increase could clearly undo the consensus that has developed, and harm national defense.[6]

One national-defense deficiency that has been virtually ignored at the levels of political leadership in the post-Afghanistan debate is the persuasive demonstration, since the abolition of the draft in the summer of 1973, that the all-volunteer forces do not provide the number or the retention ratio of trained military personnel to meet the nation's requirements for fulfilling either its strategic or its conventional defense missions. Nor is it realistic to expect these shortfalls to be overcome by increasing the financial incentives and perquisites to make national military service competitive in appeal with peacetime civilian careers. Neither is stand-by registration of draft-age youth sufficient earnest for the nation's immediate and long-term security needs.

The military draft should promptly be reinstated.

At the same time, alternative forms of national service ought to be considered, in recognition of lessons to be learned from the Vietnam era. To sustain broad public support, over a lengthy period, for substantial national-security burdens requires, not only that the public understand the reasons for sacrifice, but also that the sacrifices be equitably shared in the population.

The 1980 campaign debate was deafeningly silent, not only on the outlines of plausible U.S. strategies for the coming decade, but also on what the necessary costs will be and how the burdens should be distributed throughout the society, if the United States is to regain the power and leverage proportionate to its international responsibilities.

For more than a decade, the American people and much of the rest of the world have been distressed or bemused by U.S. shortcomings and policy failures. In both domestic and foreign policy the focus has been on the gap between the nation's proclaimed purposes and its actual performance, between its ideals and its bumbling translation of those ideals into a not-quite-workable reality, between the magnitude of America's global responsibilities and the inadequacies of U.S. leadership in carrying out those responsibilities.

A nation that a dozen years ago was criticized, at home and abroad, for arrogance of power has in recent years been accused of impotence and self-doubt about its role and purposes in the world.

These are not partisan problems, and they are not to be remedied simply by the transfer of power from one party to the other. These are problems of national self-perception, purposes, and priorities. The world's trust and confidence in America will be restored when the American people regain trust and confidence in themselves, in their ideals and institutions, and in their leadership responsibilities.

Achieving a healthy turnaround in the national mood will be no simple task for the Reagan Administration, although the gravity of the domestic and foreign challenges the nation faces provide a sobering setting for thoughtful public debate.

Deep doubts persist in many segments of the American public mind of the efficacy of a foreign policy which appears to rely solely or even primarily on an intensified confrontation of military force, to the neglect of diplomacy—or, equally important, to the neglect of urgent social and economic needs of vast numbers of the American people. Even in the aftermath of Iran, Afghanistan, and Poland, enough of the polarization of the 1970s persists to inhibit the building of a new foreign-policy consensus unless it is built on a balancing of domestic and foreign priorities, and, in global terms, a balancing of military and nonmilitary options.

A foreign policy based on fear, with too small a component of hope and aspiration, will not mobilize all the needed energies of the American people, nor will it long command their support under conditions of prolonged struggle, short of war. The mobilization of the American fighting spirit would take place instantly in the event of a clear and direct threat to the nation's security, and the spirit would stay strong until the threat was overcome. But the responsibility of America's leaders in the 1980s is not to wait for such a clear threat, but to mobilize the nation's energies in time to insure that that threat will not come.

Notes

1. Statement at the CSCE main meetings in Madrid, November 17, 1980.

2. Alexander Solzhenitsyn, "Misconceptions about Russia Are a Threat to America," *Foreign Affairs,* Spring 1980, p. 824.

3. The Reagan Administration faces special circumstances and options in Afghanistan, where it must decide whether, what kind, and how much overt or covert assistance to provide the Afghan freedom fighters, and at what risks to the Afghan peoples, to Pakistan, and indeed to broader U.S. and allied interests in Southwest Asia.

4. Soviet GNP growth rates have been declining from 6 percent in the 1950s to 5 percent in the 1960s, and 3.5 percent in the mid-1970s, and according to current CIA estimates will decline to 2.5 percent annually in the 1980s. In addition to inefficiencies in planning and management, the economy is feeling the constraints of a slowdown in growth of the labor force from 2 percent annually in the 1970–75 period to 1.5 percent since 1975, and a CIA-projected decline to 0.5 percent annual growth by 1995. Moreover, the non-Russian component of the Soviet population now exceeds 50 percent, and continues to grow more rapidly, laying the ground for possible new social tensions in Soviet society.

5. Poland's hard-currency debt to Western public and private financial institutions was estimated at $24 billion at the end of 1980, and its credit needs from the same sources for 1981 are estimated at another $11 billion.

6. Melvin R. Laird, "Not a Binge, but a Buildup," the Washington Post, November 19, 1980, p. A17.

Bibliography

Acheson, Dean. *Present at the Creation: My Years in the State Department.* New York: W. W. Norton & Co., 1965.

Ayoob, Mohammed, ed. *Conflict and Intervention in the Third World.* New York: St. Martin's Press, 1980.

Graham, Daniel O. *Shall America Be Defended: SALT II and Beyond.* New Rochelle, N.Y.: Arlington House Publishers, 1979.

Hough, Jerry F. *Soviet Leadership in Transition.* Washington, D.C.: The Brookings Institute, 1980.

Hoffman, Erik P. and Fleron, Frederick F., eds. *The Conduct of Soviet Foreign Policy.* 2nd ed. Hawthorne, N.Y.: Aldine Publishing Co., 1980.

Johnson, Lyndon Baines. *The Vantage Point: Perspectives of the Presidency, 1963-1969.* New York: Holt, Rinehart & Winston, 1971.

Kettering (Charles F.) Foundation. "Study of Public Opinion and U.S. Foreign Policy." Dayton, Ohio, 1978.

Kissinger, Henry A. *The White House Years.* Boston: Little, Brown & Co., 1979.

Newberg, Paula, ed. *United States Foreign Policy and Human Rights: Principles, Priorities, Practice.* New York: United Nations Association of U.S.A., 1979.

Nixon, Richard M. "Asia After Viet Nam." *Foreign Affairs,* 46 (1967): 111–125.

_____. *U.S. Foreign Policy for the 1970s, Building for Peace. A Report to the Congress.* Vol. 2. Washington, D.C.: U.S. Government Printing Office, 1971.

Nixon, Richard M. *U.S. Foreign Policy for the 1970s, The Emerging Structure of Peace. A Report to the Congress.* Vol. 3. Washington, D.C.: U.S. Government Printing Office, 1972.

————. *U.S. Foreign Policy for the 1970s, Shaping a Durable Peace. A Report to the Congress.* Vol. 4. Washington, D.C.: U.S. Government Printing Office, 1973.

————. *Memoirs.* New York: Grosset & Dunlap, 1978.

Pfaltzgraff, Robert L., Jr. *Energy Issues and Alliance Relationships: The United States, Western Europe and Japan.* Cambridge, Mass.: Institute for Foreign Policy Analysis, 1980.

Podhoretz, Norman. *The Present Danger.* New York: Simon & Schuster, 1980.

Solzhenitsyn, Aleksandr I. *The Mortal Danger: Misconceptions About Soviet Russia and the Threat to America.* New York: Harper & Row, 1980.

Szulc, Tad. *The Illusion of Peace—Foreign Policy in the Nixon Years.* New York: Viking Press, 1978.

Zumwalt, Elmo et al. *National Security in the 1980s: From Weakness to Strength.* Edited by W. Scott Thompson. San Francisco: Institute for Contemporary Studies, 1980.

Index

About the Author

PHILIP VAN SLYCK

is a public-affairs consultant to corporations, educational institutions, and governments, and a writer on American politics and foreign policy.

He was formerly editor of program materials for the Foreign Policy Association, and is the author of the book, *Peace: The Control of National Power*, as well as various articles, and a newsletter published in the Japanese language, *Perspective of U.S. Affairs*. He is a trustee and chairman of the executive committee of Freedom House, a trustee of the International Institute in Spain, and a member of the Asia and Japan Societies and the Commonwealth Club of California.